Long Vowel Phonics Workbook

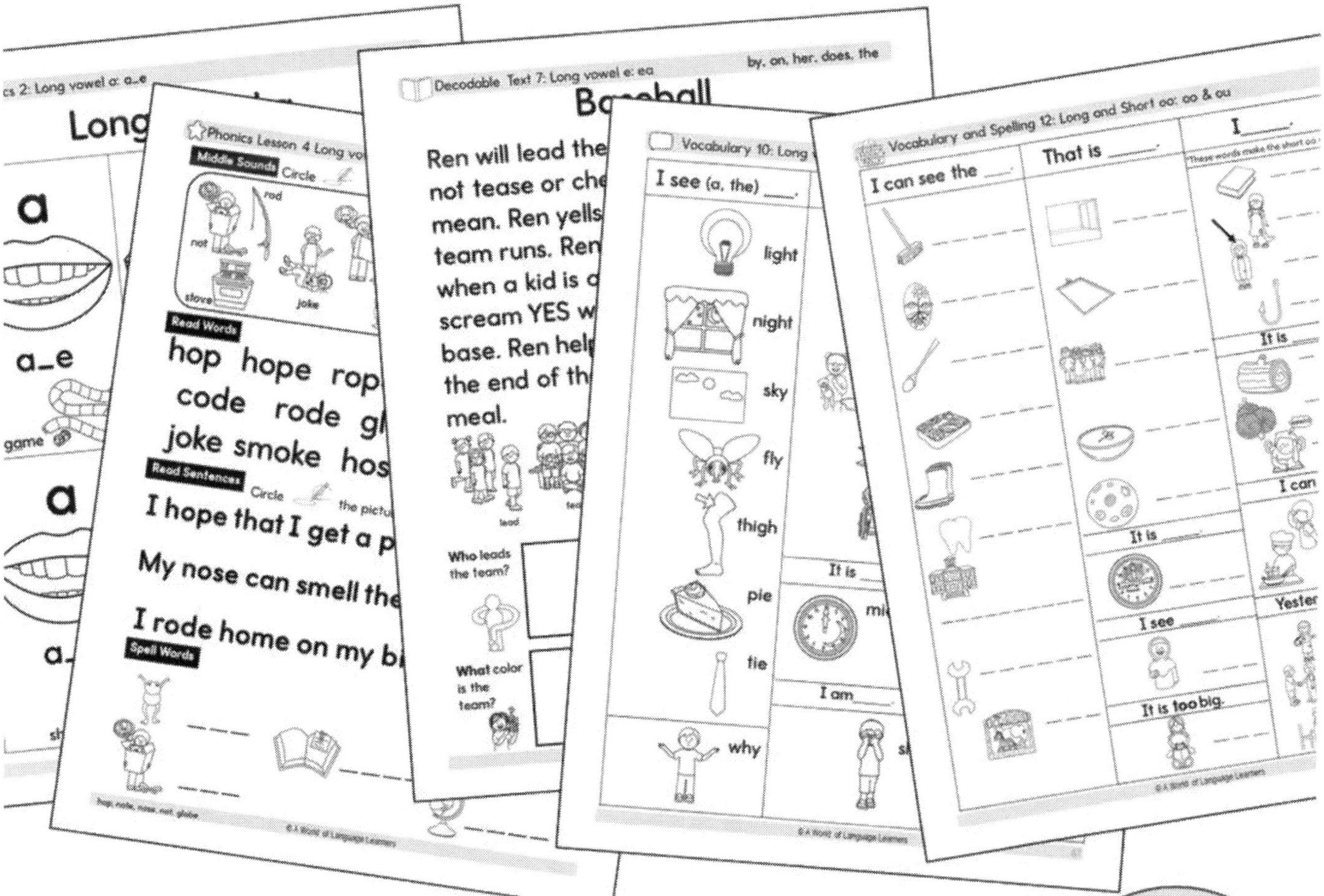

Handwriting practice, Phonics worksheets, decodable text, and vocabulary sheets

Great for older students!

Contact the author :
aworldoflanguagelearners@gmail.com

Table of Contents	Page

Instructions for Use

Newcomer English Language Learners (ELLs) come with a range of vocabulary and phonics knowledge. Some students are literate in their home language, and others do not know how to read or write in any language. This workbook is designed to be used with newcomers that need additional practice with long vowels.

There is a teacher guide for each lesson. The teacher guide gives general directions for each worksheet and has the answer key.

After the first introductory lesson, all other lessons follow the same format:

Phonics- These pages have letter cards to help introduce the new letter combinations used in the lesson.

Handwriting Practice- These pages show students how to write words and sentences that use the target sound for each lesson.

Lesson- These pages have phonemic awareness (sound) practice, reading a word, reading sentences and sometimes finding the picture that matches, and spelling words. The teacher guide tells what the pictures used are.

Decodable- The decodables give students the change to practice reading connected text using only the letters and sounds that have been introduced along with a few high frequency words. There are basic comprehension questions at the end. Either have students underline the answer in the text, say the answer out loud, or write the answer in the space included.

Vocabulary- The vocabulary page has pictures and how to spell words using only the letters and sounds that have been introduced. Tell students the names of the pictures or have them practice reading the words. You can also have students use the sentence frames to use the vocabulary words in complete sentences. This page is helpful for students to use for independent writing.

Spelling- There are the same words from the vocabulary page. There are spaces for students to practice spelling the words.

Newcomer Phonics Teacher Guide Lesson 1: Long vowels: a, i, o, u, e open syllables

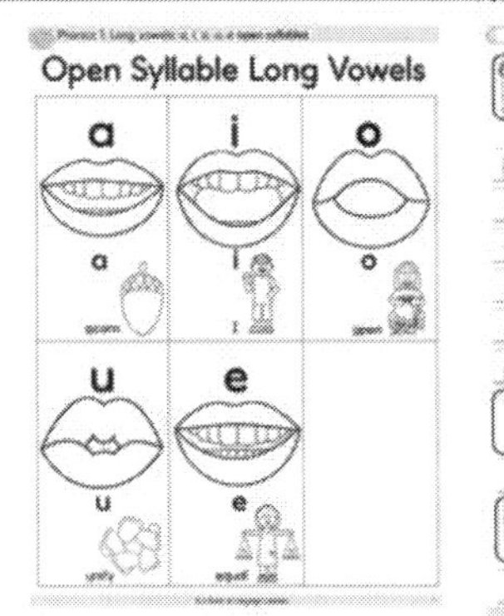

Phonics

Handwriting

Phonics: **You can clap the syllables in a word. In an open syllable the vowel sound is long. A long vowel is at the end of a syllable.**

Introduce the long vowel sounds (a, i, o, u, e)
Say the long vowel sound and key word in each space.
a acorn, i hi, o open, u unity, e equal

Handwriting: Read and point to the words in the boxes (he, she, we, me, go). Have students trace and write the words. Read the sentences and point to the pictures at the bottom of the page. (She said no. We can go.) Have students trace and write the sentences.

Lesson

Vowel Sounds
Read the words. Students circle the pictures that have a long vowel sound.
we, protect, go, me, focus, hotel, protest, silent, he, music, she
Read words
There are words with both short and long vowel sounds included.
**Additional practice: Have student underline words with a long vowel (me, we, he, she, protect, protest, go, focus, hotel, silent, music, basin)
Read sentences Circle the picture that matches the sentence. **
**Additional practice: Have student underline words with a long vowel (protect, protest, music, silent, hotel)
Spelling
go, silent, basin, we, she, protect

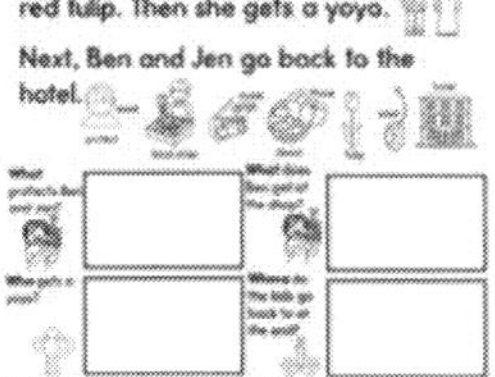

Decodable

Student reads the decodable text and then answers the comprehension questions. Review the sight words before students read the text. (soon the)

Depending on the student's language level either have them write down the answer, or say it out loud.

What protects Ben and Jan? (masks)	What does Ben get at the shop? (a frozen donut)
Who gets a yoyo? (Jan)	Where do the kids go back to at the end? (the hotel)

Vocabulary & Spelling

Vocabulary: **Student reads the decodable vocabulary words.**

Introduce the sentence frames
That is the ___. I have ___. I am ___. It is ___. I can ___. ___ can ___. It can ___.
Have the student practice using the vocabulary words in a complete sentence.

Spelling: **Student writes the word under the picture.**
If they are unsure of the word tell the student the word or have them look back to the vocabulary page.

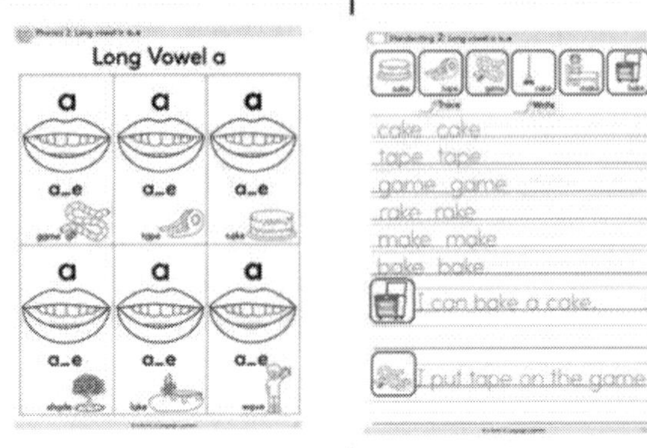

Phonics | **Handwriting**

Phonics: **When e is at the end of a word, it can make the vowel say its name.** When a word is spelled a_e the a says a and the e is silent. Say the long vowel sound and key word in each space. (a game, a tape, a cake, a shade, a lake, a wave)

Handwriting: Read and point to the words in the boxes (cake, tape, game, rake, make, bake). Have students trace and write the words. Read the sentences and point to the pictures at the bottom of the page. (I can bake a cake. I put tape on the game.) Have students trace and write the sentences.

Lesson

Middle Sounds

Read the words. Students circle the pictures that have a long vowel sound. (made, bake, tape, snake, cake, late, lake, shade, take)

Read words

There are words with both short and long vowel sounds included.

**Additional practice: Have student underline words with the long a sound (made, tape, cake, make, bake, snake, shade, take, late, lake)

Read sentences Circle the picture that matches the sentence. **

**Additional practice: Have student underline words with the long a sound (make, made, cake, hate, late)

Spelling

(mad, made, plan, plane)

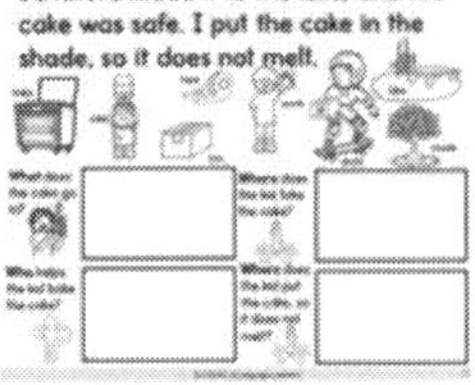

Decodable

Student reads the decodable text and then answers the comprehension questions. Review the sight words before students read the text. (soon the)

Depending on the student's language level either have them write down the answer, or say it out loud.

What does the cake go in? (in a box)	Where does the kid take the cake? (the lake)
Who helps the kid bake the cake? (dad)	Where does the kid put the cake so it will not melt? (in the shade)

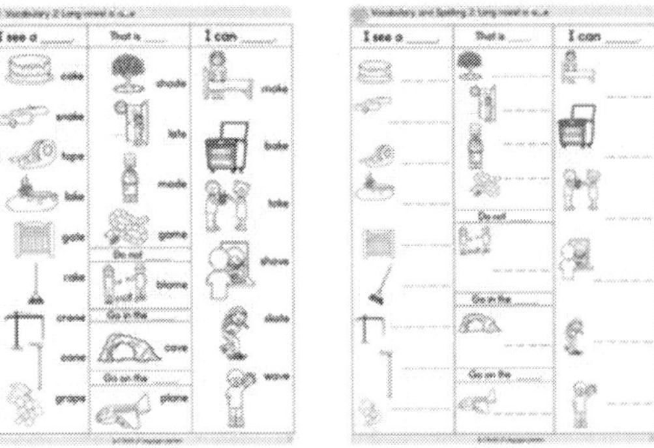

Vocabulary & Spelling

Vocabulary: **Student reads the decodable vocabulary words.**

Introduce the sentence frames

I see a ___. That is ___. Do not ___. Go in the ___. Go on the ___. I can ___.

Have the student practice using the vocabulary words in a complete sentence.

Spelling: **Student writes the word under the picture.** If they are unsure of the word tell the student the word or have them look back to the vocabulary page.

Newcomer Phonics Teacher Guide Lesson 3: Long vowels: i: i_e

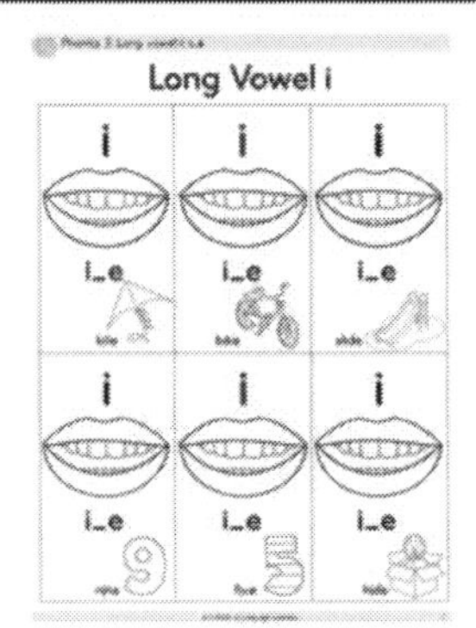

Phonics

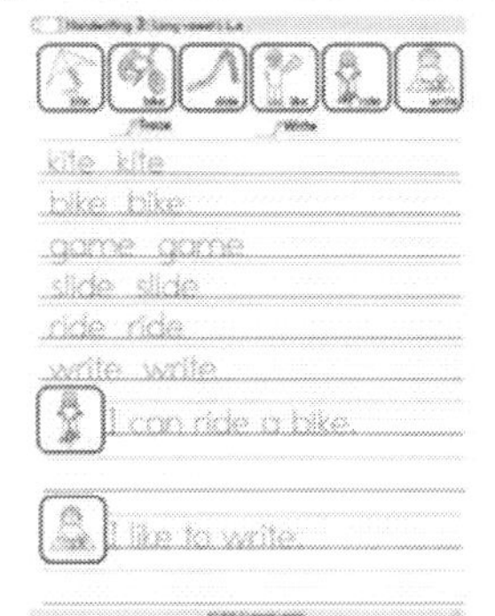

Handwriting

Phonics: **When e is at the end of a word, it can make the vowel say its name.** When a word is spelled i_e the i says i and the e is silent. Say the long vowel sound and key word in each space. (i kite, i bike, i slide, i nine, i five, i hide)

Handwriting: Read and point to the words in the boxes (kite, bike, slide, like, ride, write). Have students trace and write the words. Read the sentences and point to the pictures at the bottom of the page. (I can ride a bike. I like to write.) Have students trace and write the sentences.

Lesson

Middle Sounds

Read the words. Students circle the pictures that have a long vowel sound. (kite, five, time, hide, pile, ripe, write, ride, white, ride, slide, bite, bike)

Read words

There are words with both short and long vowel sounds included.

**Additional practice: Have student underline words with the long i sound (kite, ride, ripe, bite, bike, pile, slide, hide, five, nine, time, white, write)

Read sentences Circle the picture that matches the sentence. **

**Additional practice: Have student underline words with the long i sound (like, pile, ride, bike, five)

Spelling

(rip, ripe, bike, slide)

Decodable

Student reads the decodable text and then answers the comprehension questions. Review the sight words before students read the text. (soon the)

Depending on the student's language level either have them write down the answer, or say it out loud.

Where do the kids ride bikes? (on the sidewalk)	Where does Kim hide? (in a big pile)
Who has a white helmet? (Mike)	What is wide? (the slide)

Vocabulary & Spelling

Vocabulary: **Student reads the decodable vocabulary words.**

Introduce the sentence frames

I see (a, the)___. That is ___. I ___ that. It can ___. I can ___.

Have the student practice using the vocabulary words in a complete sentence.

Spelling: **Student writes the word under the picture.** If they are unsure of the word tell the student the word or have them look back to the vocabulary page.

Newcomer Phonics Teacher Guide Lesson 4: Long vowels: o: o_e

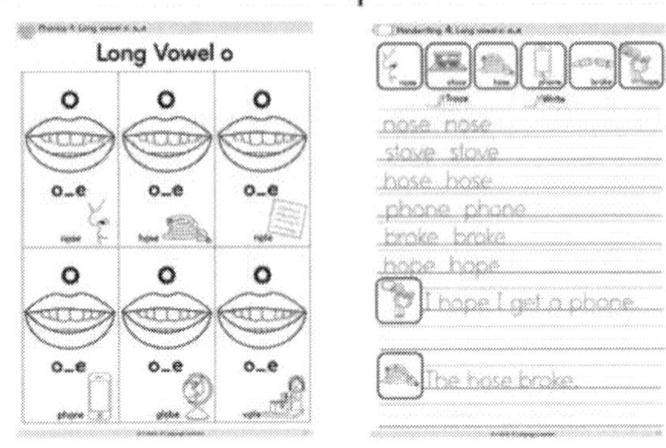

Phonics | **Handwriting**

Phonics: **When e is at the end of a word, it can make the vowel say its name.** When a word is spelled o_e the o says o and the e is silent. Say the long vowel sound and key word in each space. (o nose, o hose, o note, o phone, o globe, o vote)

Handwriting: Read and point to the words in the boxes (nose, stove, hose, phone, broke, hope). Have students trace and write the words. Read the sentences and point to the pictures at the bottom of the page. (I hope I get a phone, The hose broke.) Have students trace and write the sentences.

Lesson

Middle Sounds

Read the words. Students circle the pictures that have a long vowel sound. (stove, joke, hope, code, rode, rope, hose, home, globe, note)

Read words There are words with both short and long vowel sounds included. **Additional practice: Have student underline words with the long o sound (hope, rope, note, pole, code, rode, globe, vote, nose, joke, smoke, hose, home, stove)

Read sentences Circle the picture that matches the sentence. **

**Additional practice: Have student underline words with the long o sound (hope, nose, rode, home)

Spelling

(hop, not, note, nose, globe)

The Gift

Cole got a box. He hopes that a phone is inside the box. Cole opens the box. It is not a phone. Inside the box is a globe. The globe can spin. Cole spots a hole in the box. Cole hopes that the globe is not broken. Cole tests the globe. It can still spin! Then Cole spots a note. The note is from Rose. She wrote that the globe is a gift.

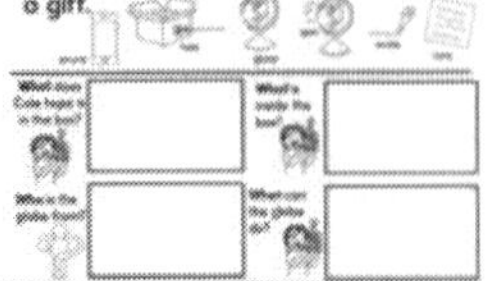

Decodable

Student reads the decodable text and then answers the comprehension questions. Review the sight words before students read the text. (soon the)

Depending on the student's language level either have them write down the answer, or say it out loud.

What does Cole hope is in the box? (a phone)	What is inside the box? (a globe)
Who is the globe from? (Rose)	What can the globe do? (it can spin)

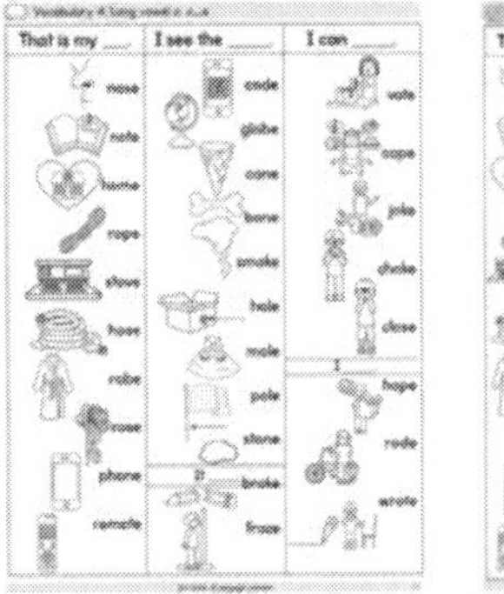

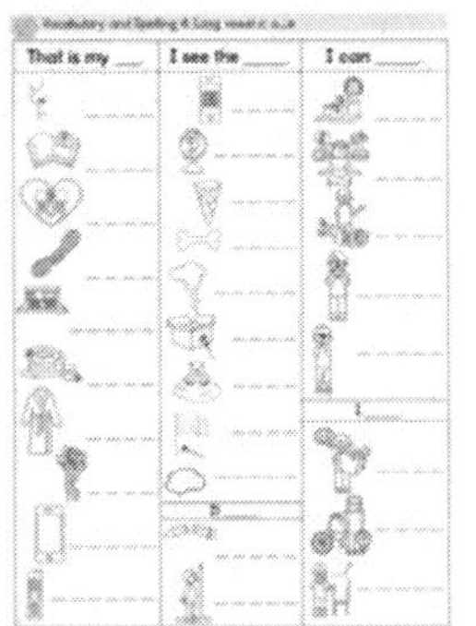

Vocabulary & Spelling

Vocabulary: **Student reads the decodable vocabulary words.**

Introduce the sentence frames

That is my ___. I see the ___. It ___. I can ___. I ___.

Have the student practice using the vocabulary words in a complete sentence.

Spelling: **Student writes the word under the picture.** If they are unsure of the word tell the student the word or have them look back to the vocabulary page.

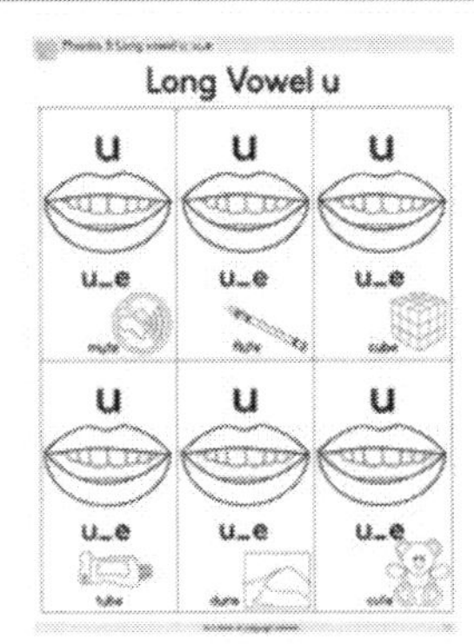

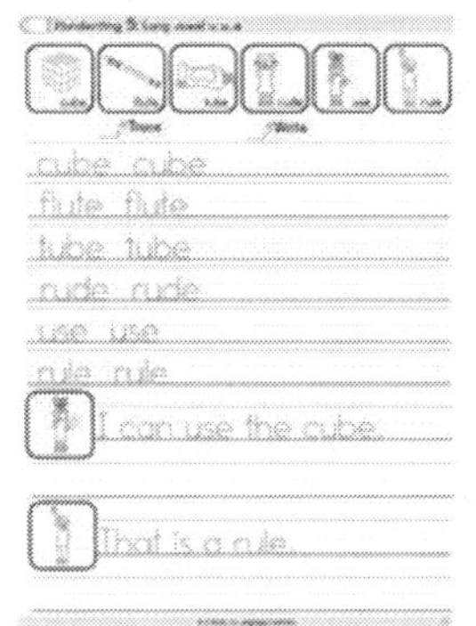

Phonics | Handwriting

Phonics: **When e is at the end of a word, it can make the vowel say its name.** When a word is spelled u_e the u says u and the e is silent. Say the long vowel sound and key word in each space. (u mute, u flute, u cube, u tube, u dune, u cube)

Handwriting: Read and point to the words in the boxes (cube, flute, tube, rude, use, rule). Have students trace and write the words. Read the sentences and point to the pictures at the bottom of the page. (I can use the cube, That is a rule.) Have students trace and write the sentences.

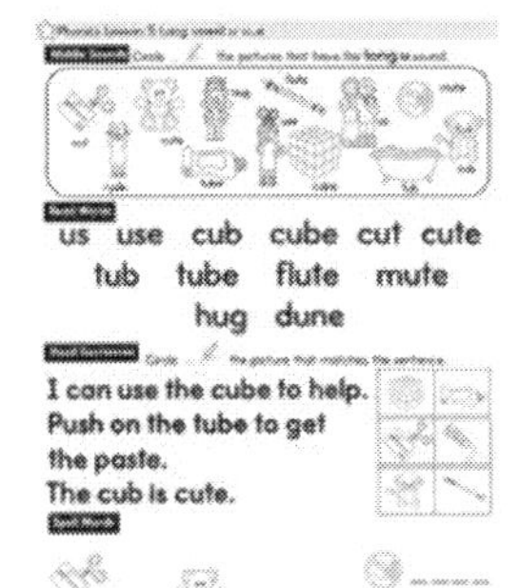

Lesson

Middle Sounds

Read the words. Students circle the pictures that have a long vowel sound. (rude, cute, tube, flute, cube, mute)

Read words There are words with both short and long vowel sounds included. **Additional practice: Have student underline words with the long o sound (use, cube, cute, tube, flute, mute, dune)

Read sentences Circle the picture that matches the sentence. **

**Additional practice: Have student underline words with the long o sound (use, cube, tube, cute)

Spelling

(cut, cute, mute, flute)

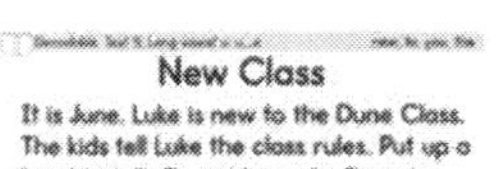

It is June. Luke is new to the Dune Class. The kids tell Luke the class rules. Put up a hand to talk. Do not be rude. Do not make excuses. The kids include Luke in the class games. The kids let Luke use the class cube. Luke can get a side of the cube red. Luke is glad he is in the Dune Class.

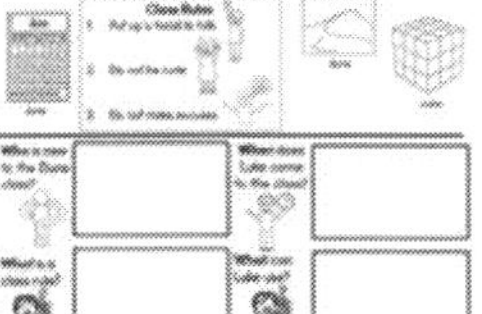

Decodable

Student reads the decodable text and then answers the comprehension questions. Review the sight words before students read the text. (soon the)

Depending on the student's language level either have them write down the answer, or say it out loud.

Who is new to the Dune class? (Luke)	When does Luke come to class? (June)
What is a class rule? (Put up a hand to talk. Do not be rude. Do not make excuses.)	What can Luke use? (the class cube)

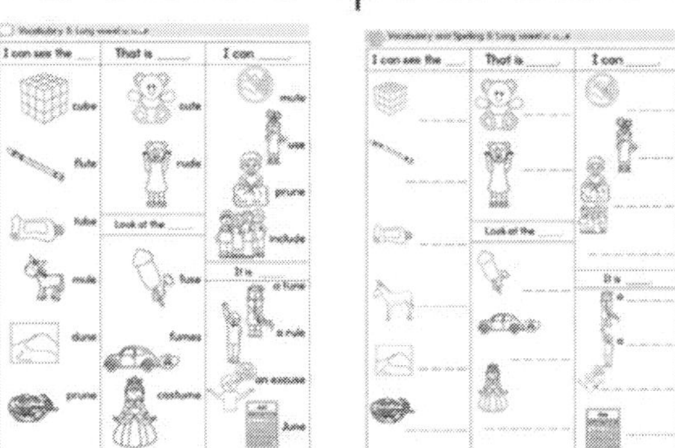

Vocabulary & Spelling

Vocabulary: **Student reads the decodable vocabulary words.**

Introduce the sentence frames

I can see the ___. That is ___. Look at the ___. I can ___. It is ___.

Have the student practice using the vocabulary words in a complete sentence.

Spelling: **Student writes the word under the picture.** If they are unsure of the word tell the student the word or have them look back to the vocabulary page.

Newcomer Phonics Teacher Guide Lesson 6: Long vowels: e: ee

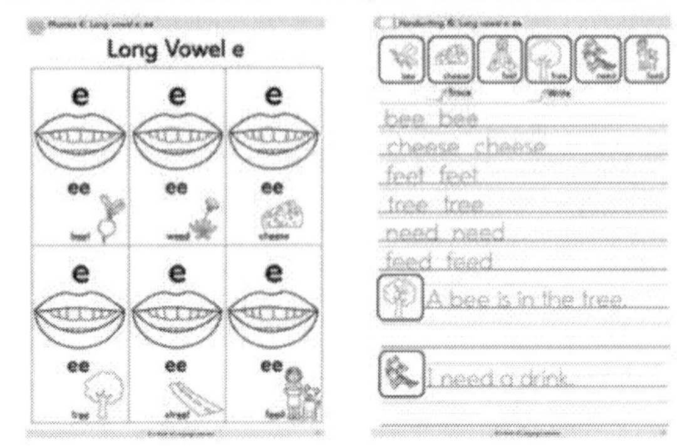

Phonics | **Handwriting**

Phonics: **ee says the long e sound.** Say the long vowel sound and key word in each space. (e beet, e weed, e cheese, e tree, e street, e feed)

Handwriting: Read and point to the words in the boxes (bee, cheese, feet, tree, need, feed). Have students trace and write the words. Read the sentences and point to the pictures at the bottom of the page. (A bee is in the tree. I need a drink.) Have students trace and write the sentences.

Lesson

Middle Sounds

Read the words. Students underline the letters that make the long e sound in each word. (ee)

Read words There are words with both short and long vowel sounds included. **Additional practice: Have student underline words with the long e sound (see, seed, feed, feet, beet, tree, green, speed, screen, sweep, weed, cheese, meet, wheel)

Read sentences Circle the picture that matches the sentence. **

**Additional practice: Have student underline words with the long e sound (green, see, feet, bee, tree)

Spelling

(see, tree, screen, feet, cheese, meet)

Decodable

Student reads the decodable text and then answers the comprehension questions. Review the sight words before students read the text. (soon the)

Depending on the student's language level either have them write down the answer, or say it out loud.

Who feeds the dog? (Lee)	Where do Bree and Lee peek? (into the kitchen)
What does Lee have as a snack? (beets)	Where does Bree sit? (with his feet in the weeds)

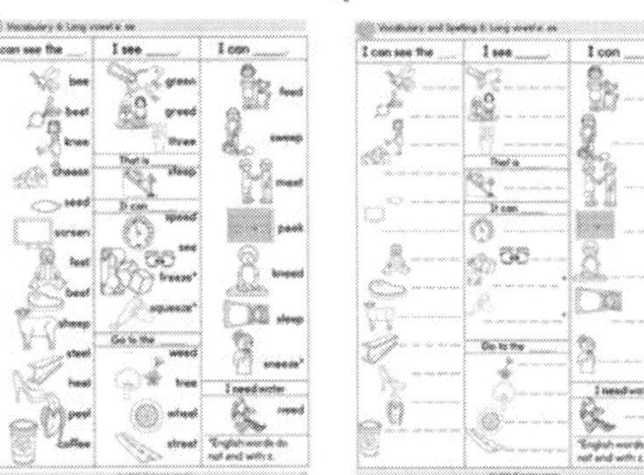

Vocabulary & Spelling

Vocabulary: **Student reads the decodable vocabulary words.**

Introduce the sentence frames

I can see the ___. I see ___. That is ___. It can ___. Go to the ___. I can ___.

Have the student practice using the vocabulary words in a complete sentence.

Spelling: **Student writes the word under the picture.** If they are unsure of the word tell the student the word or have them look back to the vocabulary page.

Newcomer Phonics Teacher Guide Lesson 7: Long vowels: e: ea

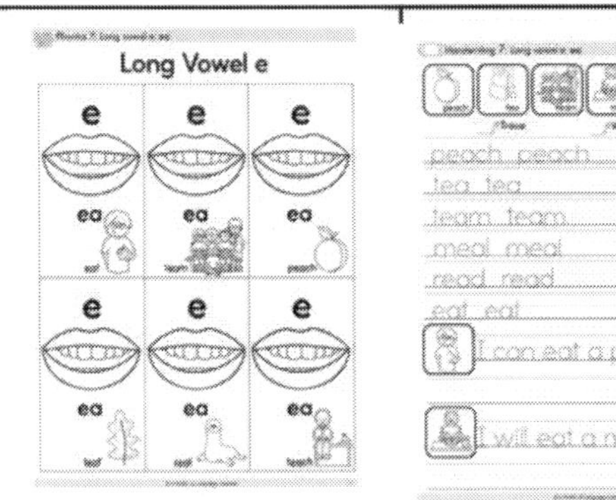

Phonics

Handwriting

Phonics: **ea says the long e sound.** Say the long vowel sound and key word in each space. (ea eat ea team ea peach ea leaf ea seal ea teach)

Handwriting: Read and point to the words in the boxes (peach tea team meal read eat). Have students trace and write the words. Read the sentences and point to the pictures at the bottom of the page. (I can eat a peach. I will eat a meal.) Have students trace and write the sentences.

Lesson

Middle Sounds

Read the words to student. Students underline the letters that make the long e sound in each word. (ea)

Read words There are words with both short and long vowel sounds included. **Additional practice: Have student underline words with the long e sound, spelled ea (eat, meat, tea, team, dream, beach, reach, leak, clean, seal, bead)

Read sentences Circle the picture that matches the sentence. **

**Additional practice: Have student underline words with the long e sound (green, see, feet, bee, tree)

Spelling

(eat, team, reach, bead, clean, mean)

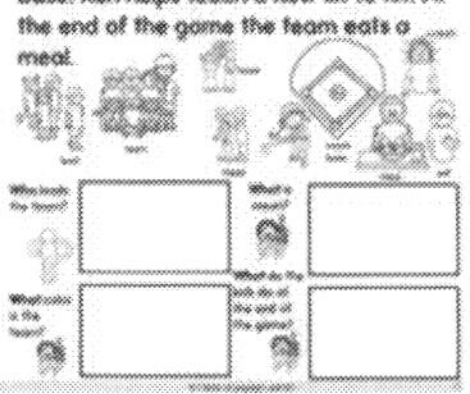

Decodable

Student reads the decodable text and then answers the comprehension questions. Review the sight words before students read the text. (soon the)

Depending on the student's language level either have them write down the answer, or say it out loud.

Who leads the team? (Ren)	What is mean? (to tease or cheat)
What color is the team? (red)	What do the kids do at the end of the game? (eat a meal)

Vocabulary & Spelling

Vocabulary: **Student reads the decodable vocabulary words.**

Introduce the sentence frames

I can see the ___. That is ___. It can ___. Go to the ___. I can ___. I should not ___.

Have the student practice using the vocabulary words in a complete sentence.

Spelling: **Student writes the word under the picture.** If they are unsure of the word tell the student the word or have them look back to the vocabulary page.

Newcomer Phonics Teacher Guide Lesson 8: Long vowels: e: ea

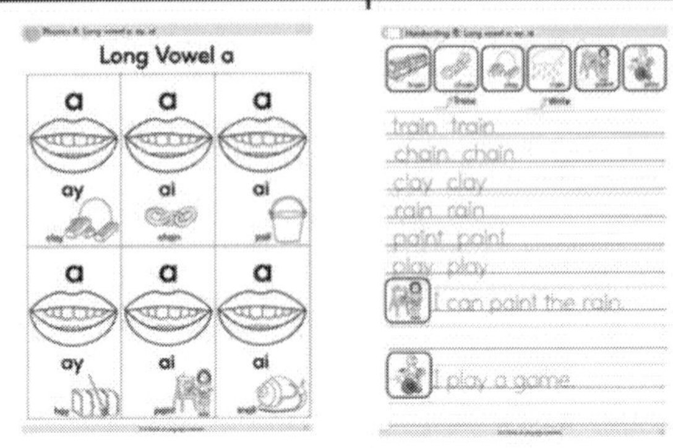

Phonics

Handwriting

<u>Phonics</u>: **ay and ai say the long a sound. Ai is found at the beginning or middle of a syllable. Ay is found at the end of a word.** Say the long vowel sound and key word in each space. (ay clay, ay clay, ai, chain, ai, paint, ai, pail, ai, snail)

<u>Handwriting</u>: Read and point to the words in the boxes (train, chain, clay, rain, paint, play). Have students trace and write the words. Read the sentences and point to the pictures at the bottom of the page. (I can paint the rain. I play a game.) Have students trace and write the sentences.

Lesson

Sounds

Say the words. Students circle where in the word they hear the long a sound. (display- end, spray- end, raise- middle, pain- middle). **Read the words to student. Students circle the pictures that have the long a sound at the end.** (pay, tray, play, lay)

Read words **Additional practice: Have student underline the letters that make the long a sound (ai, ay)

Read sentences Circle the picture that matches the sentence. **

**Additional practice: Have student underline words with the long a sound (play, rain, wait, train, stay)

Spelling

(pay, train, day, play, paint, mail)

Decodable

Student reads the decodable text and then answers the comprehension questions. Review the sight words before students read the text. (soon the)

Depending on the student's language level either have them write down the answer, or say it out loud.

Who waits for the train? (Ray)	What does Ray paint? (a display)
Where do the kids hike? (on a trail)	What is past the chain? (hay)

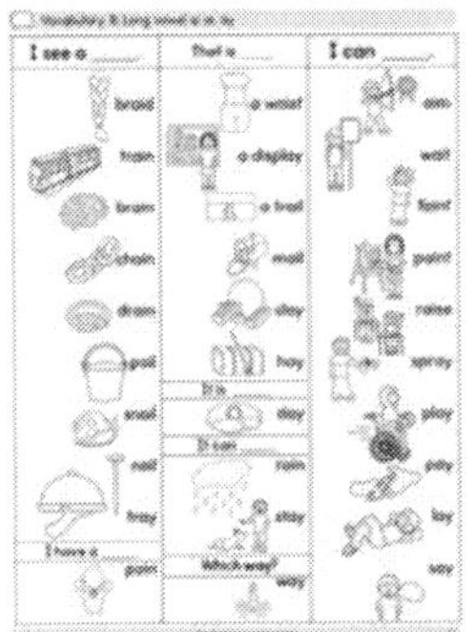

Vocabulary & Spelling

<u>Vocabulary:</u> **Student reads the decodable vocabulary words.**

Introduce the sentence frames

I see a ___. That is ___. It is ___. It can ___. I can ___.

Have the student practice using the vocabulary words in a complete sentence.

<u>Spelling:</u> **Student writes the word under the picture.** If they are unsure of the word tell the student the word or have them look back to the vocabulary page.

Newcomer Phonics Teacher Guide Lesson 9: Long vowels: o: oa, ow

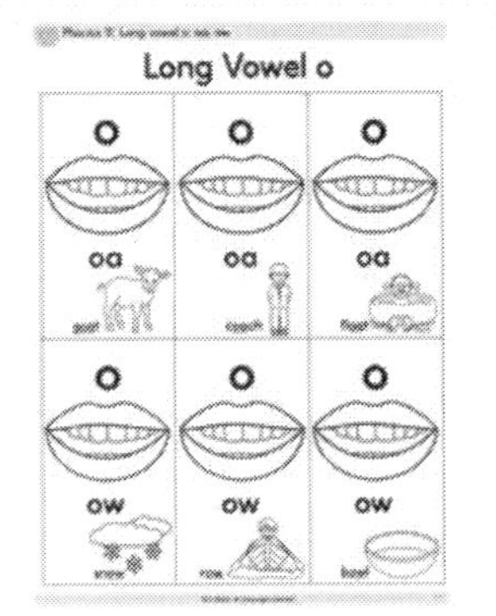

Phonics

Handwriting

Phonics: **oa and ow say the long o sound. Oa is not used at the end of a word. Ow is found in the middle or end of a word. Most of the time ow is at the end of a word.** Say the long vowel sound and key word in each space. (oa goat, oa coach, oa float, ow snow, ow row, ow bowl)

Handwriting: Read and point to the words in the boxes (snow, road, soap, bowl, coat, throat). Have students trace and write the words. Read the sentences and point to the pictures at the bottom of the page. (Snow is on the road. He put on a coat.) Have students trace and write the sentences.

boat goat toast
tow mow snow
coach road elbow
float blow show

I must mow the grass.
The tow truck is on the road.
That goat is in the snow.

Lesson

Sounds: Say the words. Students circle where in the word they hear the long o sound. (throat- middle, soap- middle, throw- end, oak- beginning).
Read the words to the student. Students circle the pictures that have the long o sound at the end. (tow, show, blow, mow, elbow, snow)
Read words **Additional practice: Have student underline the letters that make the long o sound (ow, oa).
Read sentences Circle the picture that matches the sentence.
**Additional practice: Have student underline words with the long o sound (mow, tow, road, goat, snow)
Spelling (snow, goat, soap, throw, road, elbow)

Camp

The kids go to camp. Sam floats on the lake. Pam rows a boat. The coach shows the kids how to aim a bow and arrow. Do not hit the oak tree! Down the road the kids can see a goat, a sheep, and a tree frog. The goat and the sheep drink out of a bowl. One day it snows. The camp is closed.

Decodable

Student reads the decodable text and then answers the comprehension questions. Review the sight words before students read the text. (soon the)

Depending on the student's language level either have them write down the answer, or say it out loud.

Who floats on the lake? (Sam)	What does the coach do? (show the kids how to aim a bow and arrow)
Where does the sheep get a drink? (a bowl)	What happens when it snows? (camp is closed)

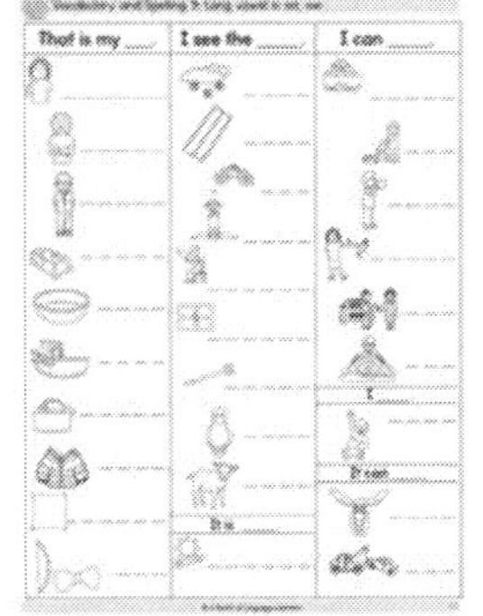

Vocabulary & Spelling

Vocabulary: **Student reads the decodable vocabulary words.**

Introduce the sentence frames
That is my ___. I see the ___. It is ___. I can ___. I ___. It can ___.
Have the student practice using the vocabulary words in a complete sentence.

Spelling: **Student writes the word under the picture.** If they are unsure of the word tell the student the word or have them look back to the vocabulary page.

Newcomer Phonics Teacher Guide Lesson 10: Long vowels: e: ea

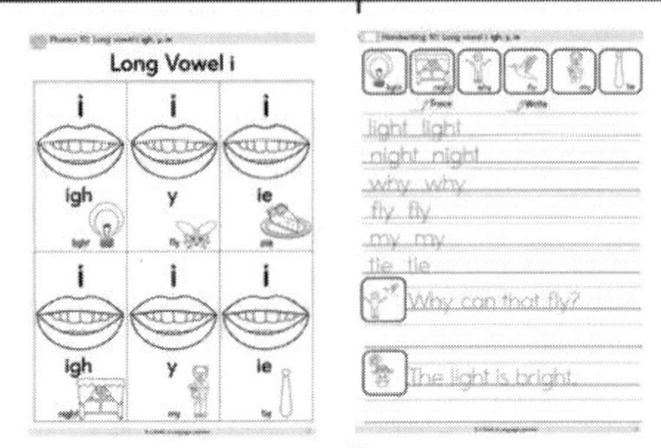

Phonics

Handwriting

Phonics: **igh, y, and ie say the long i sound. Igh is found in the middle or end of a word. Y is found at the end of a word or syllable when it makes the long I sound. Ie is found at the end of a word.** (only 4 words use ie, die, pie, lie, tie. Ie is also used when a suffix is added to words ending in y). Say the long vowel sound and key word in each space. (igh light, igh, night, y fly, y my, ie pie, ie tie)

Handwriting: Read and point to the words in the boxes (light, night, why, fly, my, tie). Have students trace and write the words. Read the sentences and point to the pictures at the bottom of the page. (Why can that fly? The light is bright.) Have students trace and write the sentences.

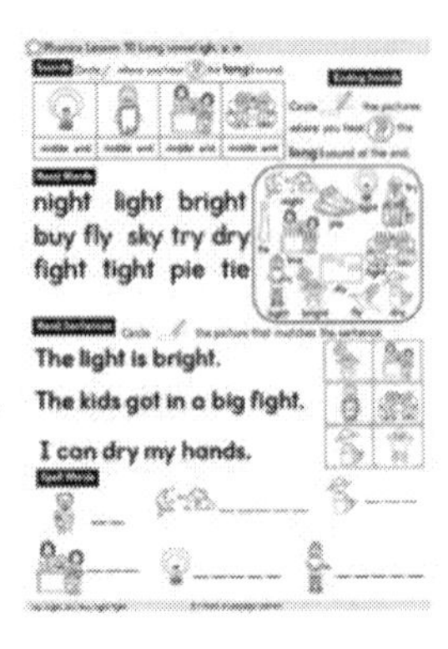

Lesson

Sounds: Say the words. Students circle where in the word they hear the long i sound. (light- middle, right- middle, buy- end, fight- middle). **Read the words to the student. Students circle the pictures that have the long i sound at the end.** (tie, buy, pie, sky, fly, dry, try)

Read words **Additional practice: Have student underline the letters that make the long i sound (igh, y, ie).

Read sentences Circle the picture that matches the sentence.

**Additional practice: Have student underline words with the long i sound (light, bright, fight, dry)

Spelling

(my, night, dry, buy, light, tight)

The Babysitter

Milo has a job. He helps with Pip. Pip is not shy of Milo. Milo gets a fly out of the crib. He stops the bright light. He puts Pip into the crib to sleep. At midnight Pip gets up. The sky is dark. What will Milo try? Milo picks Pip up high. Milo puts Pip back into the crib. No luck. Milo gets Pip pie. Pip does not cry. Pip eats the pip. Then Pip goes back to sleep. Pie was just right for Pip.

Decodable

Student reads the decodable text and then answers the comprehension questions. Review the sight words before students read the text. (soon the)

Depending on the student's language level either have them write down the answer, or say it out loud.

Who does Milo help with? (Pip)	Where is the fly? (in the crib)
What happens at midnight? (Pip gets up)	What helps Pip go back to sleep? (pie)

Vocabulary & Spelling

Vocabulary: **Student reads the decodable vocabulary words.**

Introduce the sentence frames

I see (a, the)___. That is ___. It is ___. I am ___. I can ___. Go to the ___. It can ___.

Have the student practice using the vocabulary words in a complete sentence.

Spelling: **Student writes the word under the picture.** If they are unsure of the word tell the student the word or have them look back to the vocabulary page.

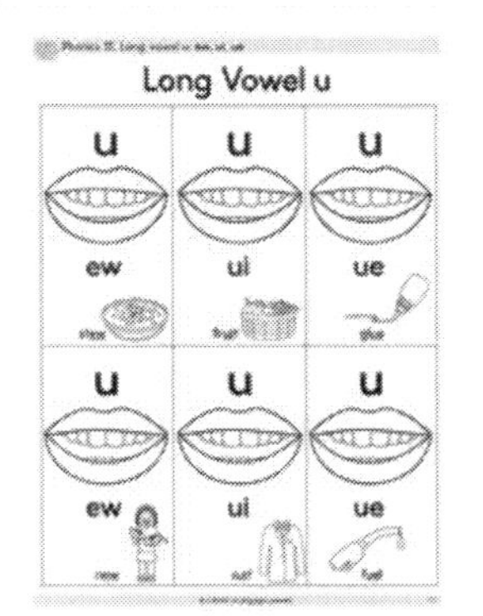

Phonics

Handwriting

Phonics: **ew, ui, ue say the long u sound. Ew is usually found at the end of a word or syllable.** Say the long vowel sound and key word in each space. (ew stew, ew new, ui fruit, ui suit, ue glue, ue fuel)

Handwriting: Read and point to the words in the boxes (blue, fruit, glue, drew, suit, suitcase). Have students trace and write the words. Read the sentences and point to the pictures at the bottom of the page. (I drew blue fruit. The suitcase has a suit.) Have students trace and write the sentences.

few flew new news grew
drew crew screw fruit glue
blew blue stew chew cashew
The plant grew.
Chew the cashew nut.
I drew the crew.

Lesson

Sounds

Read the words to students. Students underline the letters that make the long u sound in each word. (ew)

Read words **Additional practice: Have student underline the letters that make the long u sound (ew, ui, ue).

Read sentences Circle the picture that matches the sentence. **

**Additional practice: Have student underline words with the long e sound (grew, chew, cashew, drew, crew)

Spelling

(few, new, chew, flew, news, crew)

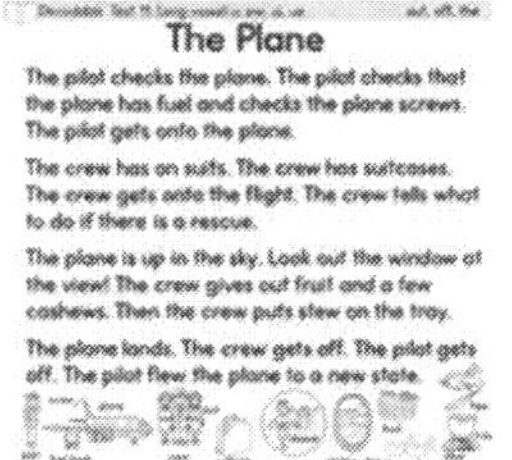
The Plane

The pilot checks the plane. The pilot checks that the plane has fuel and checks the plane screws. The pilot gets onto the plane.

The crew has on suits. The crew has suitcases. The crew gets onto the flight. The crew tells what to do if there is a rescue.

The plane is up in the sky. Look out the window at the view! The crew gives out fruit and a few cashews. Then the crew puts stew on the tray.

The plane lands. The crew gets off. The pilot gets off. The pilot flew the plane to a new state.

Decodable

Student reads the decodable text and then answers the comprehension questions. Review the sight words before students read the text. (soon the)

Depending on the student's language level either have them write down the answer, or say it out loud.

Who checks the plane? (pilot)	What does the crew have on? (suits)
What does the crew give out? (fruit and a few cashews)	Where did the plane land? (in a new state)

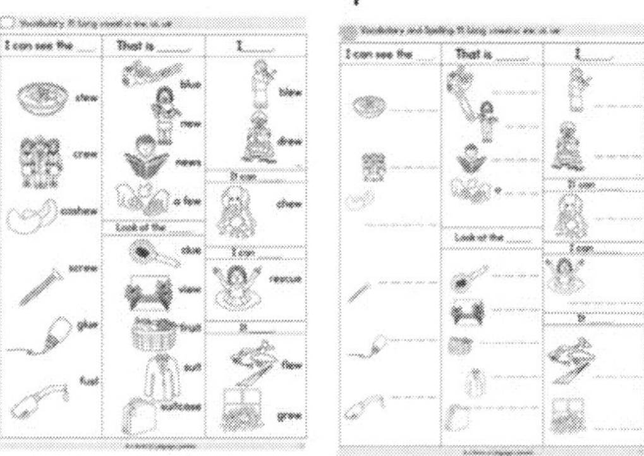

Vocabulary & Spelling

Vocabulary: **Student reads the decodable vocabulary words.**

Introduce the sentence frames

I can see the ___. That is ___. Look at the ___. I ___. It can ___. I can ___. It ___.

Have the student practice using the vocabulary words in a complete sentence.

Spelling: **Student writes the word under the picture.** If they are unsure of the word tell the student the word or have them look back to the vocabulary page.

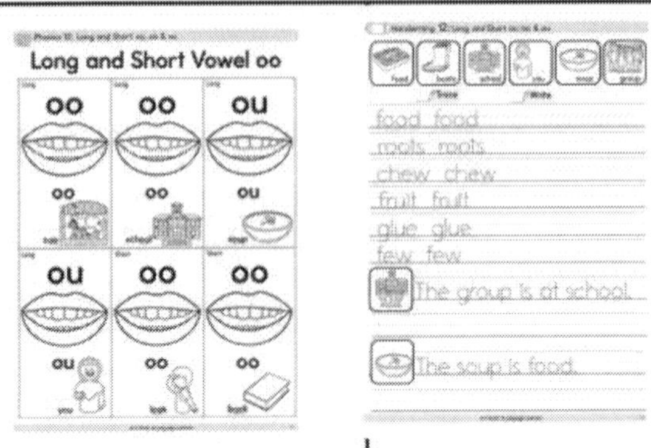

Phonics

Handwriting

Phonics: **oo and ou can say the long or short oo sound.** Say the long oo vowel sound and key word in each space. (oo zoo, oo school, oo you, oo look) . Say the short oo vowel sound and key word in each space. (oo look, oo book)

Handwriting: Read and point to the words in the boxes (food boots, school, you, soup, group). Have students trace and write the words. Read the sentences and point to the pictures at the bottom of the page. (The group is at school. The soup is food.) Have students trace and write the sentences.

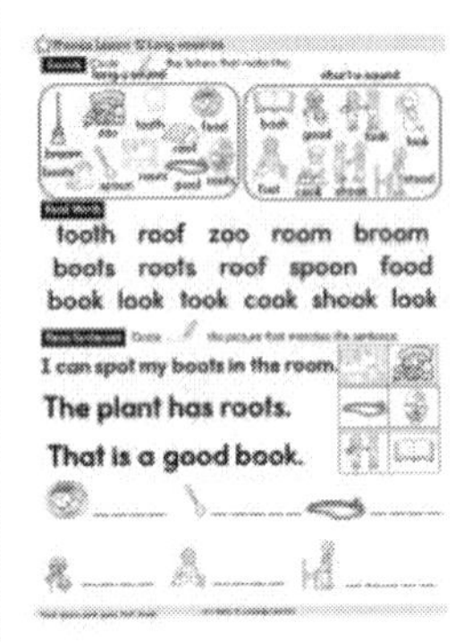

Lesson

Long and Short Sounds

Read the words to students. Students circle the letters that make the long or short oo sound in each word. (oo).

Read words There are words with both short and long oo sounds included. **Additional practice: Have student underline words with the long oo sound, spelled ea (tooth, roof, zoo, room, broom, boots, roots, roof, spoon, food)

Read sentences Circle the picture that matches the sentence. **

**Additional practice: Have student underline words with the long oo sound (roots)

Spelling

(food, spoon, pool, good, foot, stood)

Decodable

Student reads the decodable text and then answers the comprehension questions. Review the sight words before students read the text. (soon the)

Depending on the student's language level either have them write down the answer, or say it out loud.

Where do the kids go at noon? (the zoo)	Who looks at roots? (the blue group)
What does the green group look at? (a big tooth)	Where are the ducks? (on a wood log)

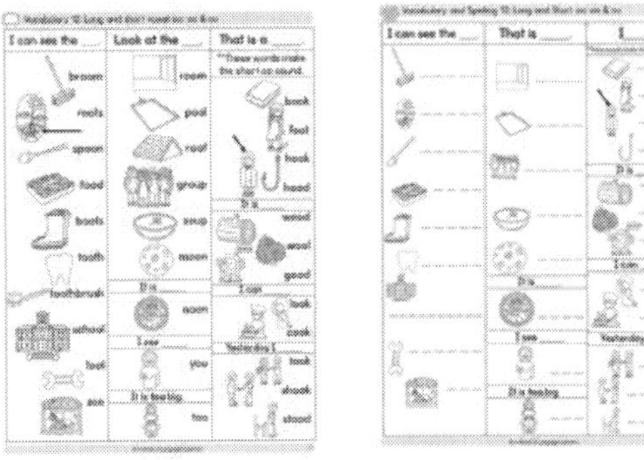

Vocabulary & Spelling

Vocabulary: **Student reads the decodable vocabulary words.**

Introduce the sentence frames

I can see the ___. That is ___. It is ___. I see___. I ___. I can ___. Yesterday I ___.

Have the student practice using the vocabulary words in a complete sentence.

Spelling: **Student writes the word under the picture.** If they are unsure of the word tell the student the word or have them look back to the vocabulary page.

Newcomer Phonics Teacher Guide Lesson 13: Hard and Soft c and g

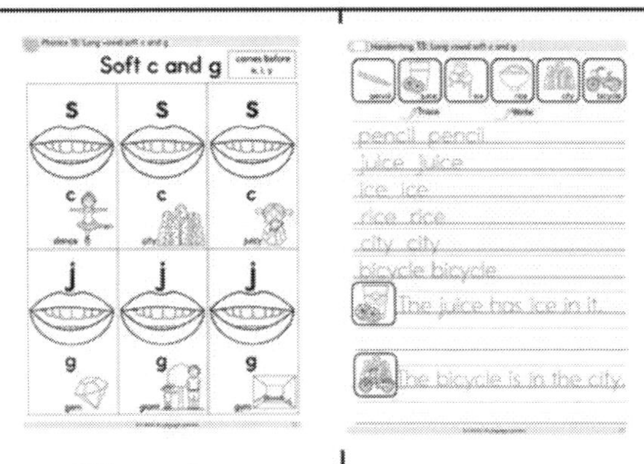

Phonics | **Handwriting**

Phonics: **c and make the /s/ sound when c comes before e, i, y.** Say the /s/ sound spelled with c and key word in each space. (c dance, c city, c juicy). **g and make the /j/ sound when c comes before e, i, y.** Say the /j/ sound spelled with g and key word in each space. (g gem, g giant, g gym).

Handwriting: Read and point to the words in the boxes (pencil, juice, ice, rice, city, bicycle). Have students trace and write the words. Read the sentences and point to the pictures at the bottom of the page. (The juice has ice in it. The bicycle is in the city.) Have students trace and write the sentences.

Lesson

Middle Sounds

Read the words. Students underline the letters that make the long e sound in each word. (ea)

Read words There are words with soft and hard g and j sounds included.

**Additional practice: Have student underline c and g when those letters are making the /s/ or /j/ sounds. (face, rice, ice, city, cycle, juice, gem, giant, age, cage, bridge, package, bicycle.

Read sentences Circle the picture that matches the sentence. **

**Additional practice: Have student underline c and g when those letters are making the /s/ or /j/ sounds. (bicycle, bridge, package, juice)

Spelling

(rice, face, ice, gem, age, package)

Decodable

Student reads the decodable text and then answers the comprehension questions. Review the sight words before students read the text. (soon the)

Depending on the student's language level either have them write down the answer, or say it out loud.

Who dances? (Jene)	Where does she dance? (the center of the stage)
What is on the dress? (lace)	What does Jene ride? (a bicycle)

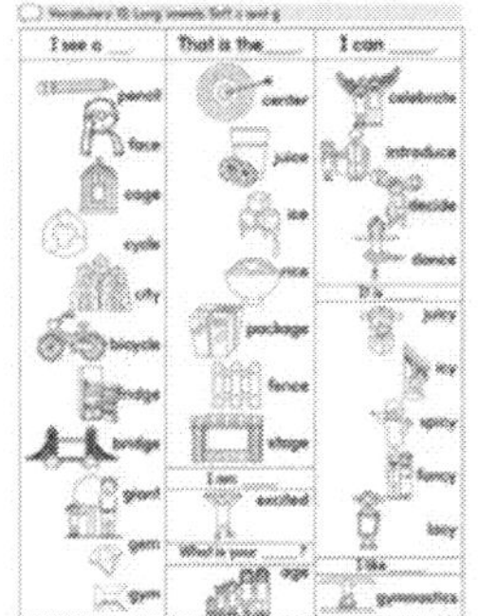

Vocabulary & Spelling

Vocabulary: **Student reads the decodable vocabulary words.**

Introduce the sentence frames

I can see the ___. That is ___. It can ___. Go to the ___. I can ___. I should not ___.

Have the student practice using the vocabulary words in a complete sentence.

Spelling: **Student writes the word under the picture.**
If they are unsure of the word tell the student the word or have them look back to the vocabulary page.

Open Syllable Long Vowels

a	i	o
a acorn	i I	o open
u	e	
u unity	e equal	

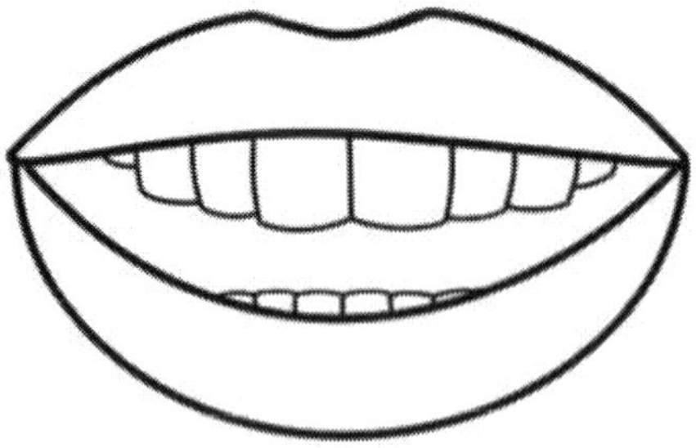

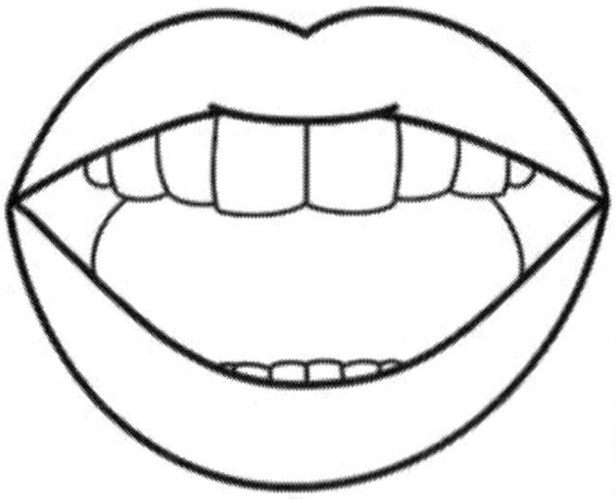

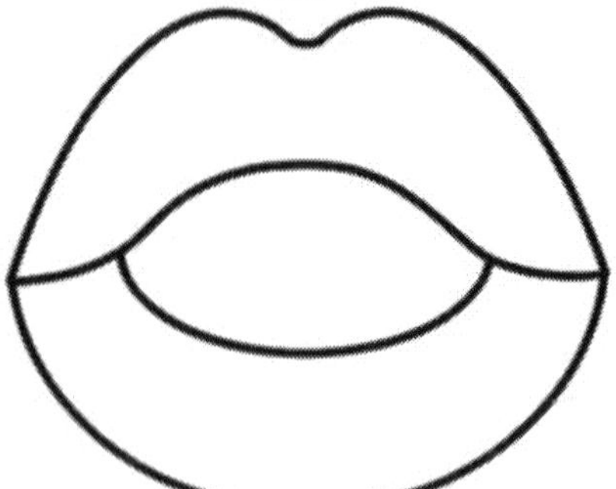

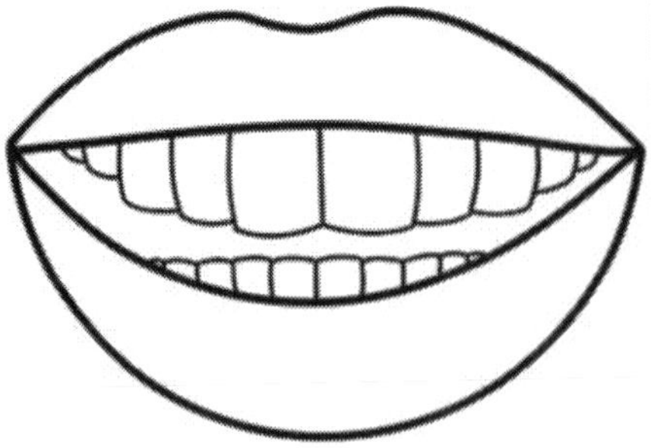

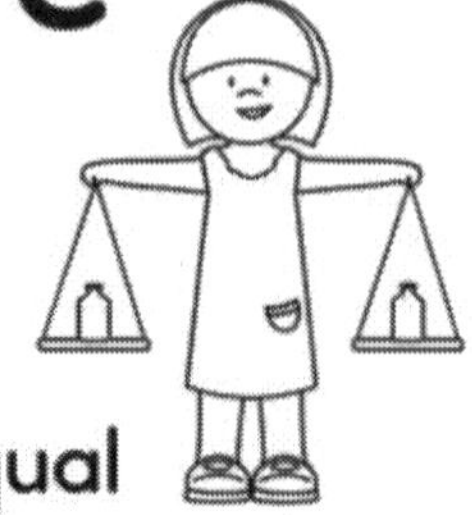

Handwriting 1: Long vowels: a, i, o, u, e open syllables

he she we me go no

Trace Write

he he

she she

we we

me me

go go

no no

She said no.

We can go.

Open Syllables

Vowel Sounds Circle the pictures that have the **long vowel** sound.

Read Words

me met we wet he hen she shed

protect protest go got focus

hotel silent sit music mug basin

Read Sentences Circle the picture that matches the sentence.

A mask can protect me.

The protest had music.

It is silent at the hotel.

Spell Words

 __ __   __ __ __ __ __ __  __ __ __ __ __

 __ __  __ __ __  __ __ __ __ __ __ __

go, silent, basin, we, she, protect

The Shop

I am Ben. I am Jan.

We go to a local shop. We put on masks to protect us. The shop is silent. No music is on.

At the shop, Ben gets a donut. He gets a frozen donut. Jen gets a red tulip. Then she gets a yoyo.

Next, Ben and Jen go back to the hotel.

Vocabulary 1: Long vowels: a, i, o, u, e open syllables

That is the ___.	I am ___.	___ can ___.
basin hotel music tulip donut yoyo	silent	we he she I
	It is ___.	
	local frozen	
	It is so big. so	I can ___.
	No, I can not. no	go focus protest open
I have ___.	Be on time. be	
zero	Look at ___.	It can ___.
hi Hi, nice to see you	me	protect

That is the ___.	I am ___.	___ can ___.
_ _ _ _ _	_ _ _ _ _ _	_ _
_ _ _ _ _	**It is ___.**	_ _
_ _ _ _ _	_ _ _ _ _	_ _ _
_ _ _ _ _	_ _ _ _ _ _ _	**I can ___.**
_ _ _ _ _	It is _ _ big.	_ _
_ _ _ _	_ _ _	_ _ _ _ _
I have ___.	_ _ , I can not.	_ _ _ _ _ _ _
_ _ _ _	_ _	**It can ___.**
Hi, nice to see you	_ _ on time.	_ _ _ _ _ _ _
_ _	_ _	**Look at ___.**
	_ _ _ _ _ _ I can.	_ _
	_ _ _ _ _	

Long Vowel a

a a_e game	a a_e tape	a a_e cake
a a_e shade	a a_e lake	a a_e wave

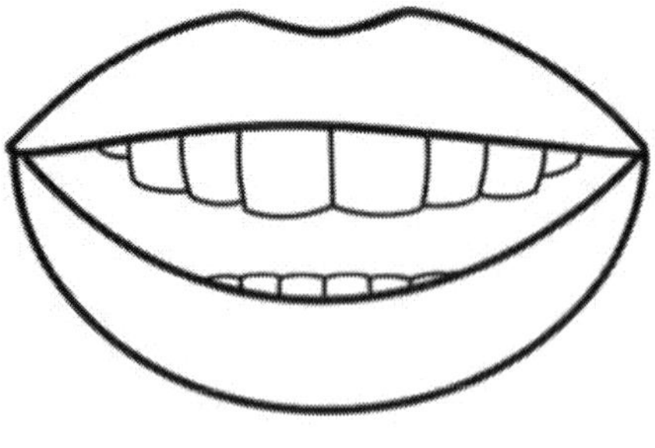

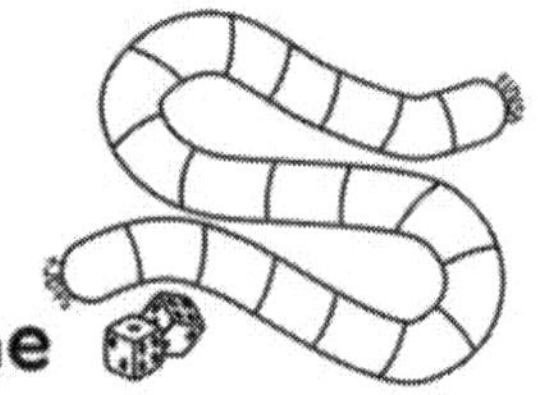

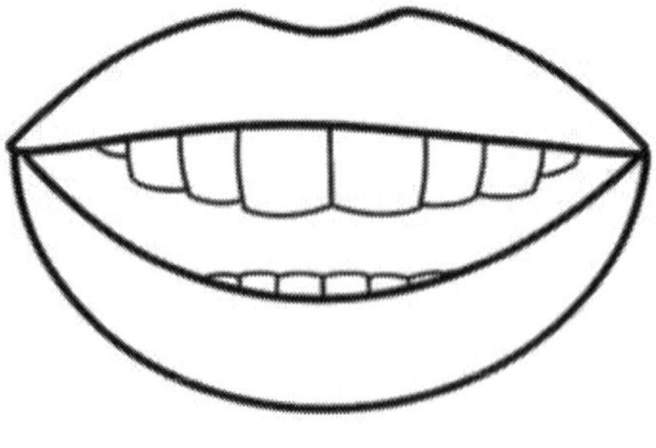

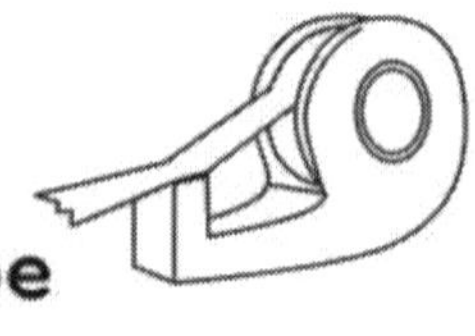

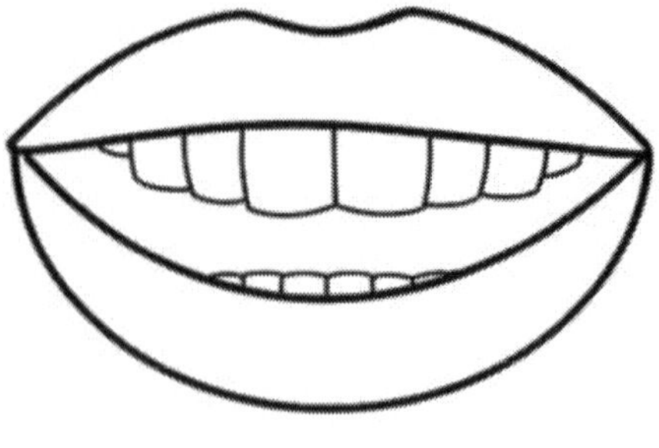

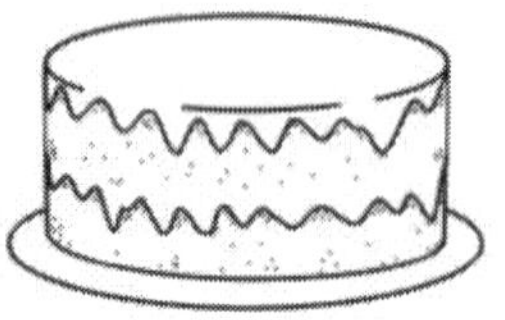

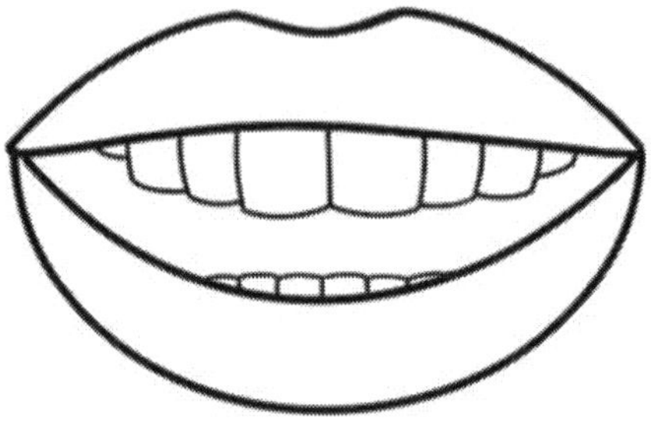

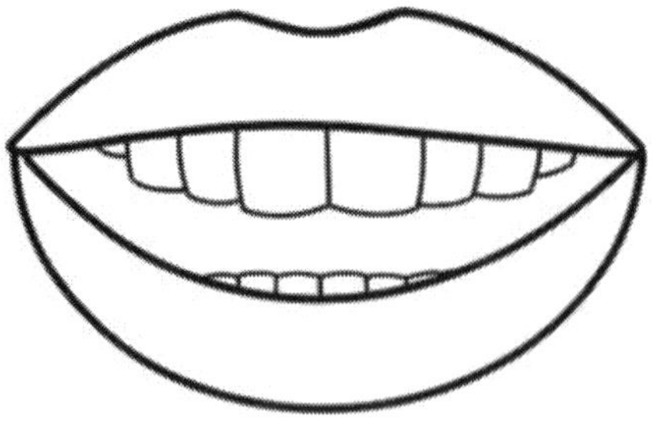

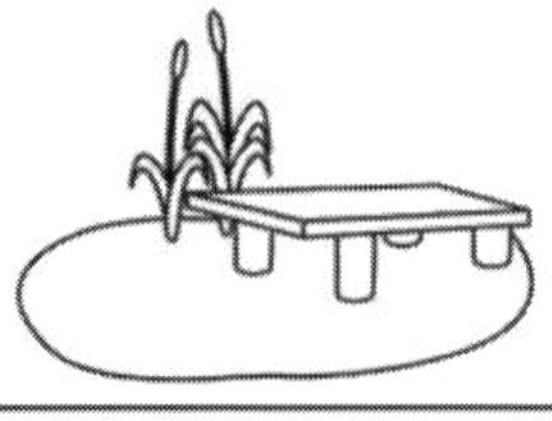

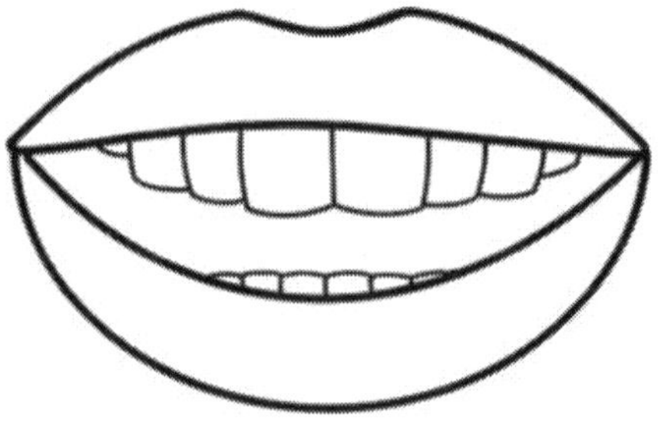

Handwriting 2: Long vowel a: a_e

cake tape game rake make bake

Trace

Write

cake cake

tape tape

game game

rake rake

make make

bake bake

I can bake a cake.

I put tape on the game.

Phonics Lesson 2 Long vowel a_e

Middle Sounds Circle the pictures that have the **long a** sound.

Read Words

mad made nap tape hat

can cake make bake

snake shade take late lake

Read Sentences Circle  the picture that matches the sentence.

The kid can make a snack.

The man made a big cake.

I hate when I am late.

Spell Words

_ _ _

_ _ _ _

_ _ _ _

_ _ _ _ _

The Cake

I made a cake with Dad to take to the lake. I had to mix. Dad helped bake to make the cake. I put the cake in a box. I put tape on top of the cake box. I wave to Mom. Then I skate to the lake. I must not drop the cake. I must not be late. I made it to the lake, and the cake was safe. I put the cake in the shade, so it does not melt.

What does the cake go in?

Who helps the kid bake the cake?

Where does the kid take the cake?

Where does the kid put the cake, so it does not melt?

Vocabulary 2: Long vowel a: a,_e

I see a _____.	That is ____.	I can _____.
cake	shade	make
snake	late	bake
tape	made	take
lake	game	shave
gate	**Do not ____.**	skate
rake	blame	wave
crane	**Go in the ____.**	
cane	cave	
grape	**Go on the ____.**	
	plane	

I see a _____.	That is _____.	I can _____.
_ _ _ _	_ _ _ _ _	_ _ _ _
_ _ _ _ _	_ _ _ _	_ _ _ _
_ _ _ _	_ _ _ _	_ _ _ _
_ _ _ _	_ _ _ _	_ _ _ _ _
_ _ _ _	**Do not _____.**	_ _ _ _ _
_ _ _ _	_ _ _ _ _	_ _ _ _
_ _ _ _ _	**Go in the _____.**	
_ _ _ _	_ _ _ _	
_ _ _ _ _	**Go on the _____.**	
	_ _ _ _ _	

Long Vowel i

i i_e kite	i i_e bike	i i_e slide
i i_e nine	i i_e five	i i_e hide

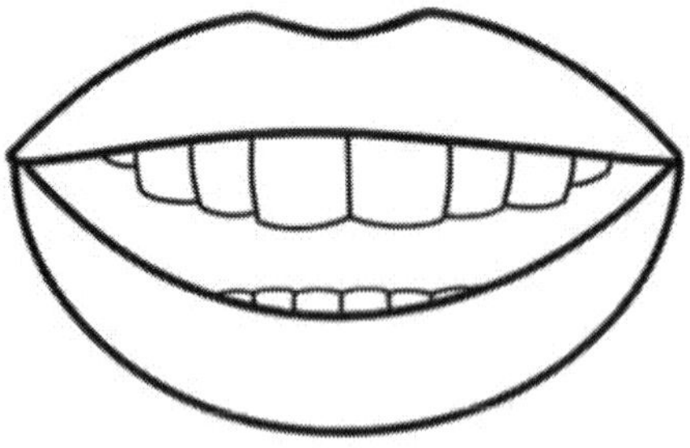

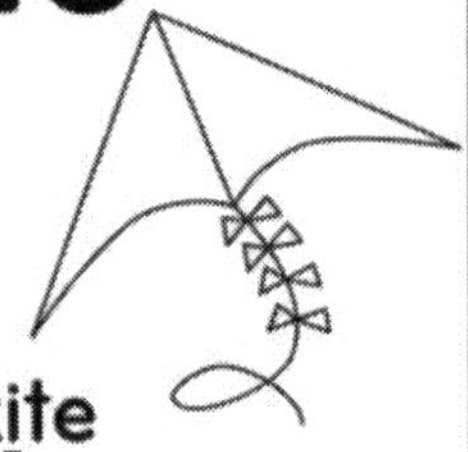

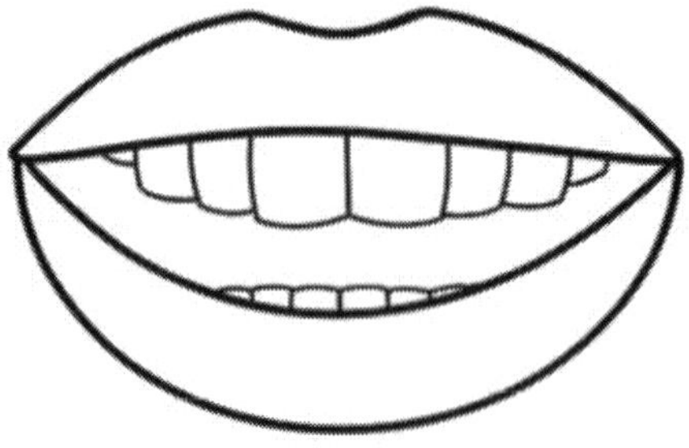

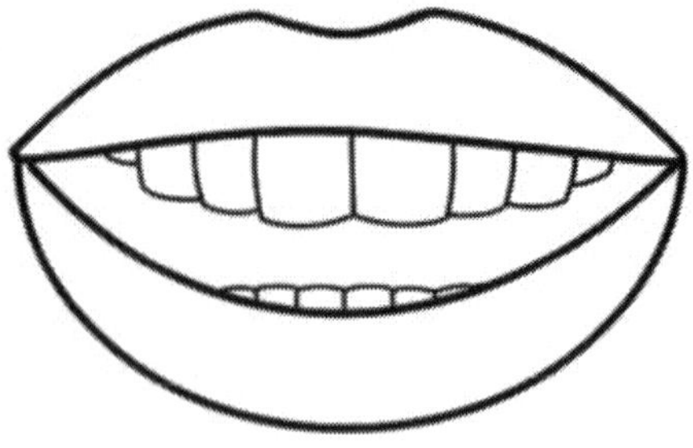

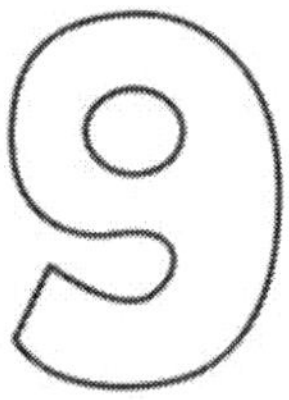

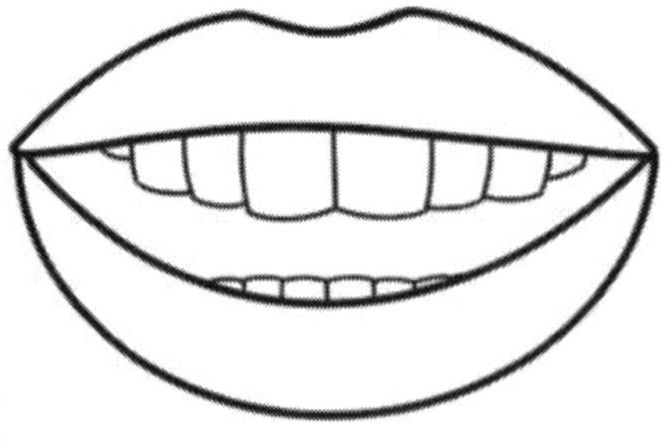

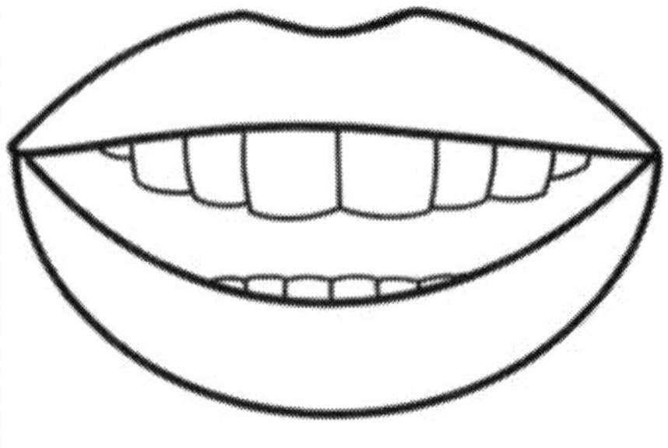

Handwriting 3: Long vowel i: i_e

kite bike slide like ride write

Trace Write

kite kite

bike bike

game game

slide slide

ride ride

write write

I can ride a bike.

I like to write.

Middle Sounds  Circle the pictures that have the **long i** sound.

Read Words

kit kite rid ride rip ripe

bite bike pill pile slide hide

five nine time white write

Read Sentences  Circle  the picture that matches the sentence.

I like to jump in the big pile.

The kid can ride a bike.

The kit has five pins.

Spell Words

 _ _ _

 _ _ _ _

 _ _ _ _

 _ _ _ _

The Bike Ride

The kids ride bikes on the sidewalk. Mike has a white helmet, and Kim has a pink helmet. Mike spots a slide. The slide is wide. The kids slide. Next, Kim says find me. Kim hides in a big pile. Mike finds her. Then, it is time to get back on the bikes to ride.

Where do the kids ride bikes?

Where does Kim hide?

Who has a white helmet?

What is wide?

Vocabulary 3: Long vowel i: i,_e

I see (a, the) ___.	That is ____.	I can _____.
kite	white	ride
pile	ripe	write
slide	a site	hide
bike	wide	dive
nine	I like that.	glide
five	It can ____.	hike
prize	bite	
dime		
lime		
sidewalk		

I see (a, the) ___.	That is ___.	I can ___.
_ _ _ _	_ _ _ _ _	_ _ _ _
_ _ _ _	_ _ _ _	_ _ _ _ _
_ _ _ _ _	a _ _ _ _	_ _ _ _
_ _ _ _	_ _ _ _	_ _ _ _
_ _ _ _	**I _ _ _ _ that.**	_ _ _ _
_ _ _ _	_ _ _ _	_ _ _ _
_ _ _ _ _	**It can ___.**	
_ _ _ _	_ _ _ _	
_ _ _ _		
_ _ _ _ _ _ _ _		

Long Vowel o

o o_e nose	o o_e hose	o o_e note
o o_e phone	o o_e globe	o o_e vote

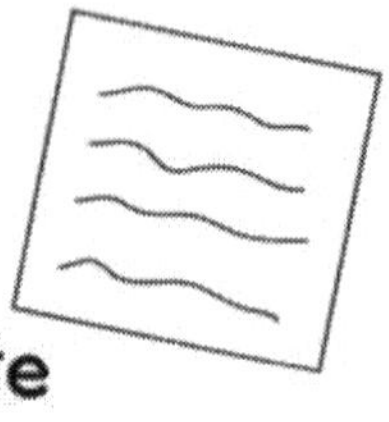

Handwriting 4: Long vowel o: o_e

nose stove hose phone broke hope

Trace Write

nose nose

stove stove

hose hose

phone phone

broke broke

hope hope

I hope I get a phone.

The hose broke.

Phonics Lesson 4 Long vowel o_e

Middle Sounds Circle the pictures that have the **long o** sound.

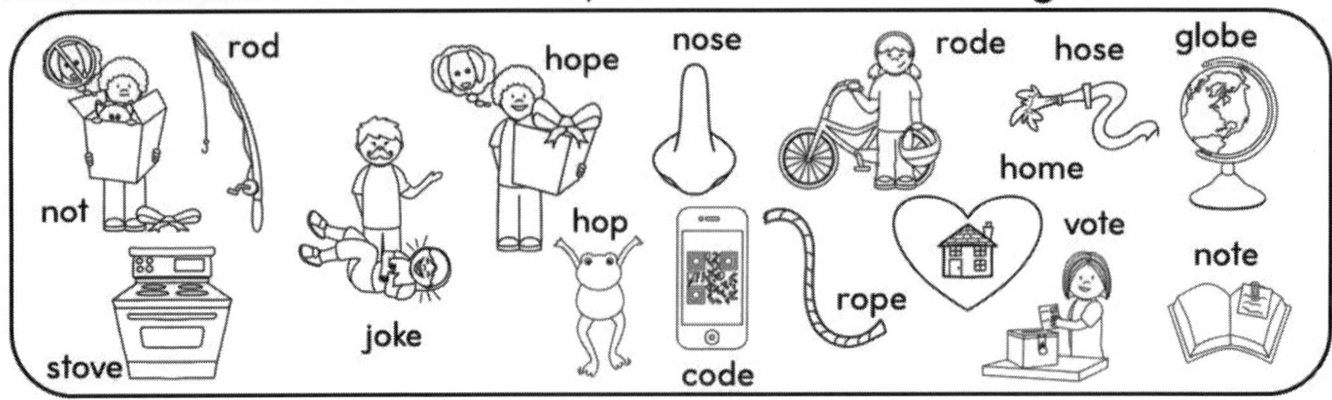

Read Words

hop hope rope not note pole

code rode globe vote nose

joke smoke hose home stove

Read Sentences Circle   the picture that matches the sentence.

I hope that I get a pet dog.

My nose can smell the cake.

I rode home on my bike.

Spell Words

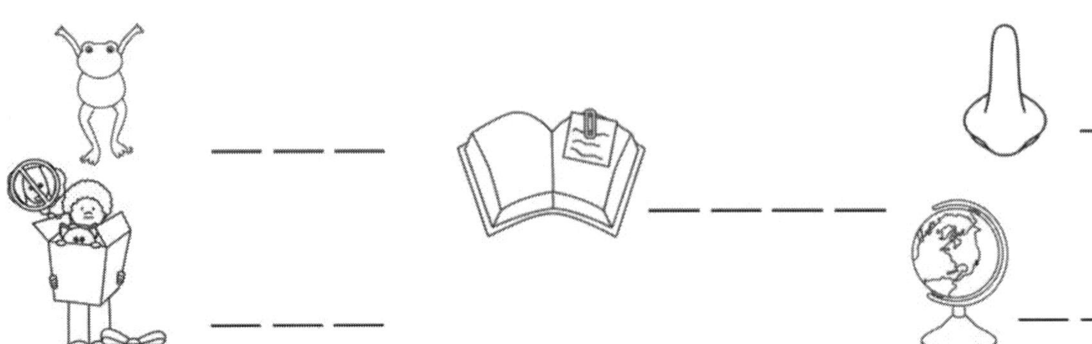

___ ___ ___

___ ___ ___ ___

___ ___ ___ ___

___ ___ ___

___ ___ ___ ___ ___

The Gift

Cole got a box. He hopes that a phone is inside the box. Cole opens the box. It is not a phone. Inside the box is a globe. The globe can spin. Cole spots a hole in the box. Cole hopes that the globe is not broken. Cole tests the globe. It can still spin! Then Cole spots a note. The note is from Rose. She wrote that the globe is a gift.

Vocabulary 4: Long vowel o: o_e

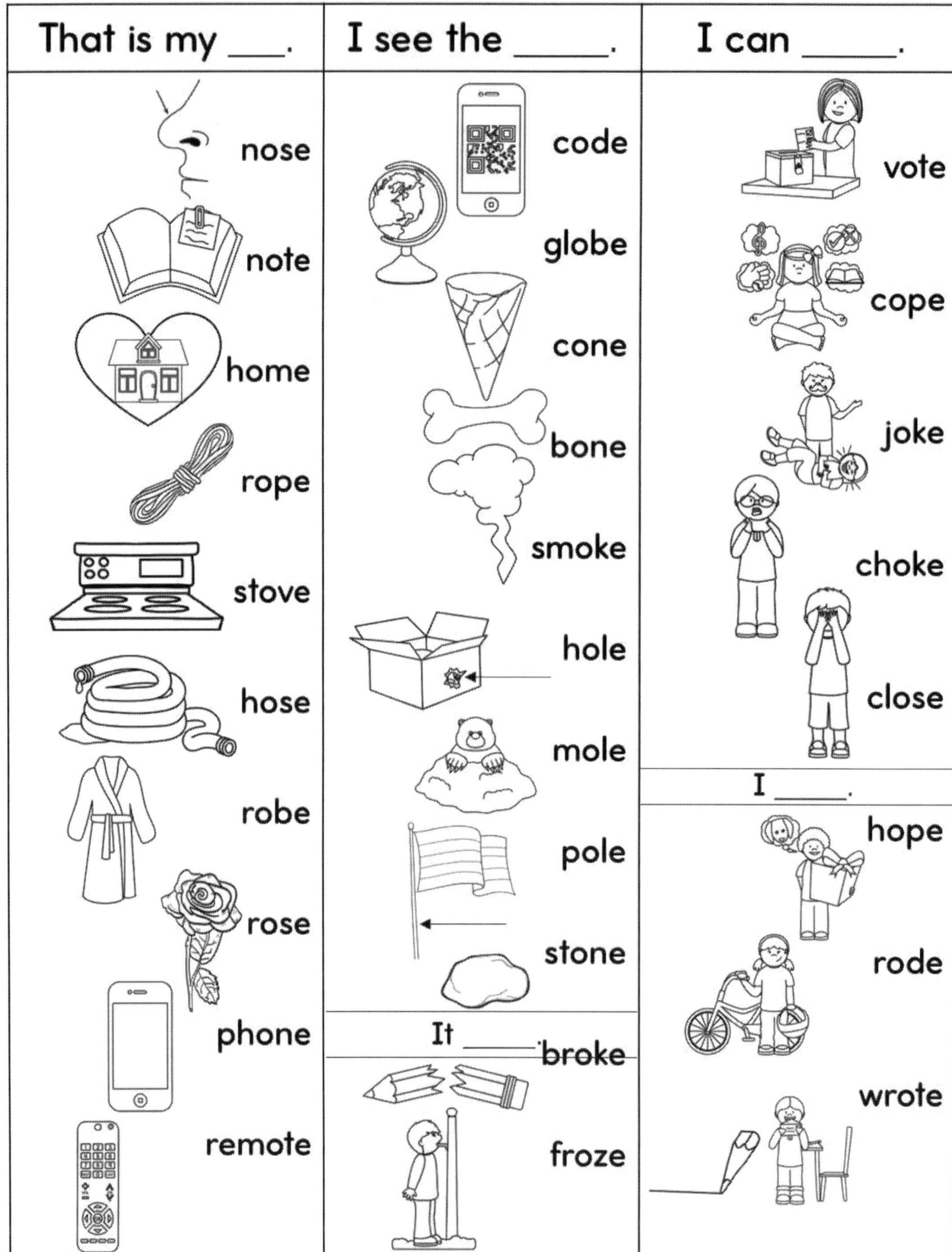

That is my ___.	I see the _____.	I can _____.
nose	code	vote
note	globe	cope
home	cone	joke
rope	bone	choke
stove	smoke	close
hose	hole	**I ____.**
robe	mole	hope
rose	pole	rode
phone	stone	wrote
remote	**It ____.**	
	broke	
	froze	

Vocabulary and Spelling 4: Long vowel o: o,_e

That is my ___.	I see the _____.	I can _____.
__ __ __ __	__ __ __ __	__ __ __ __
__ __ __ __	__ __ __ __ __	__ __ __ __
__ __ __ __	__ __ __ __	__ __ __ __
__ __ __ __	__ __ __ __	__ __ __ __ __
__ __ __ __ __	__ __ __ __ __	__ __ __ __ __
__ __ __ __	__ __ __ __	**I _____.**
__ __ __ __	__ __ __ __	__ __ __ __
__ __ __ __	__ __ __ __	__ __ __ __
__ __ __ __	__ __ __ __ __	__ __ __ __ __
__ __ __ __ __ __	**It _____.**	
	__ __ __ __ __	
	__ __ __ __ __	

Long Vowel u

u u_e mute	u u_e flute	u u_e cube
u u_e tube	u u_e dune	u u_e cute

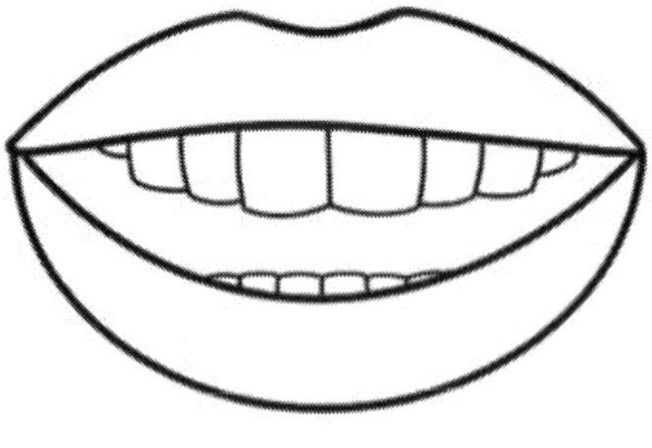

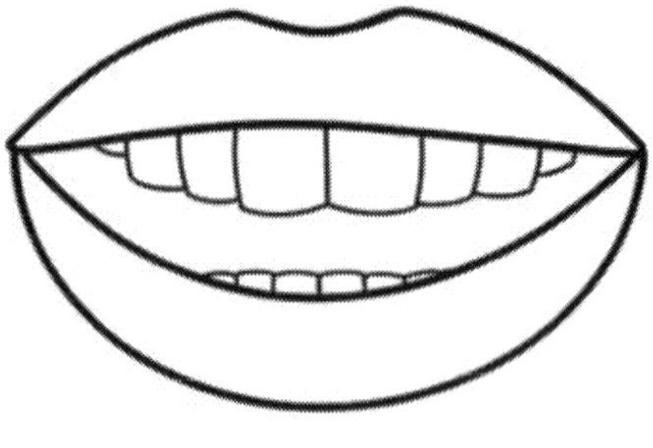

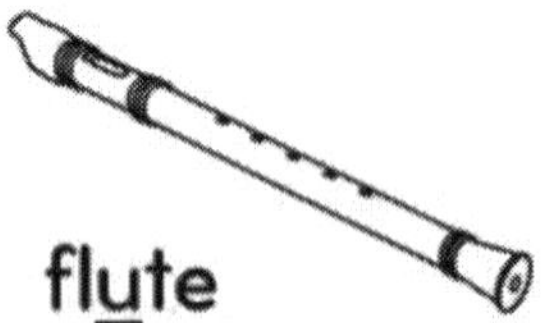

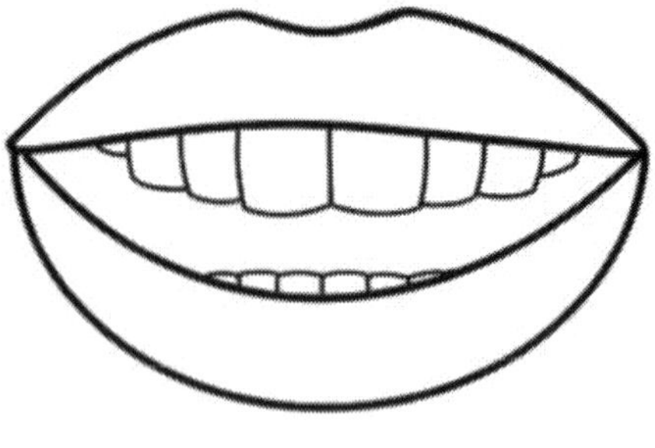

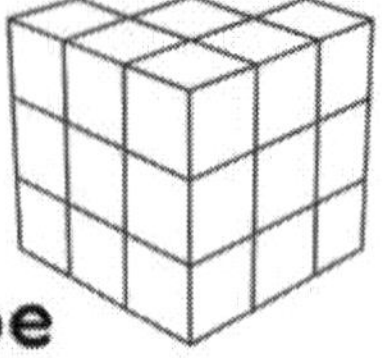

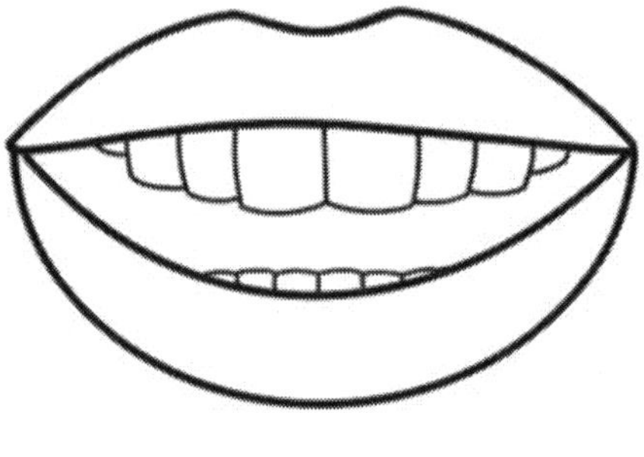

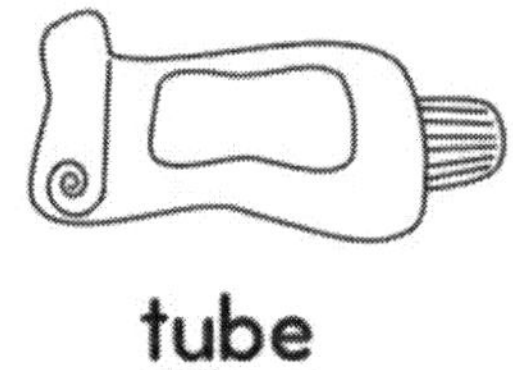

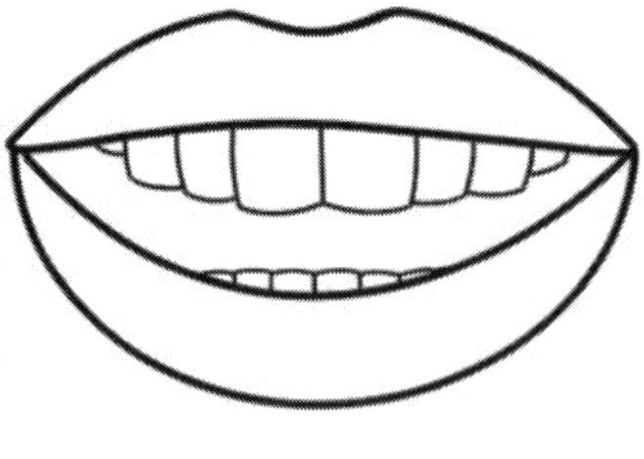

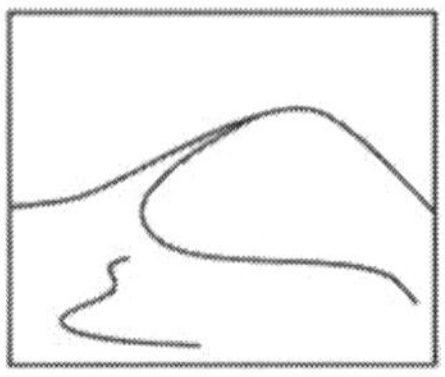

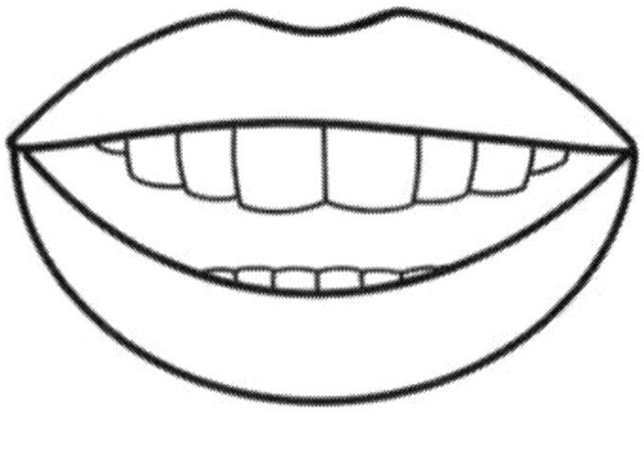

Handwriting 5: Long vowel u: u_e

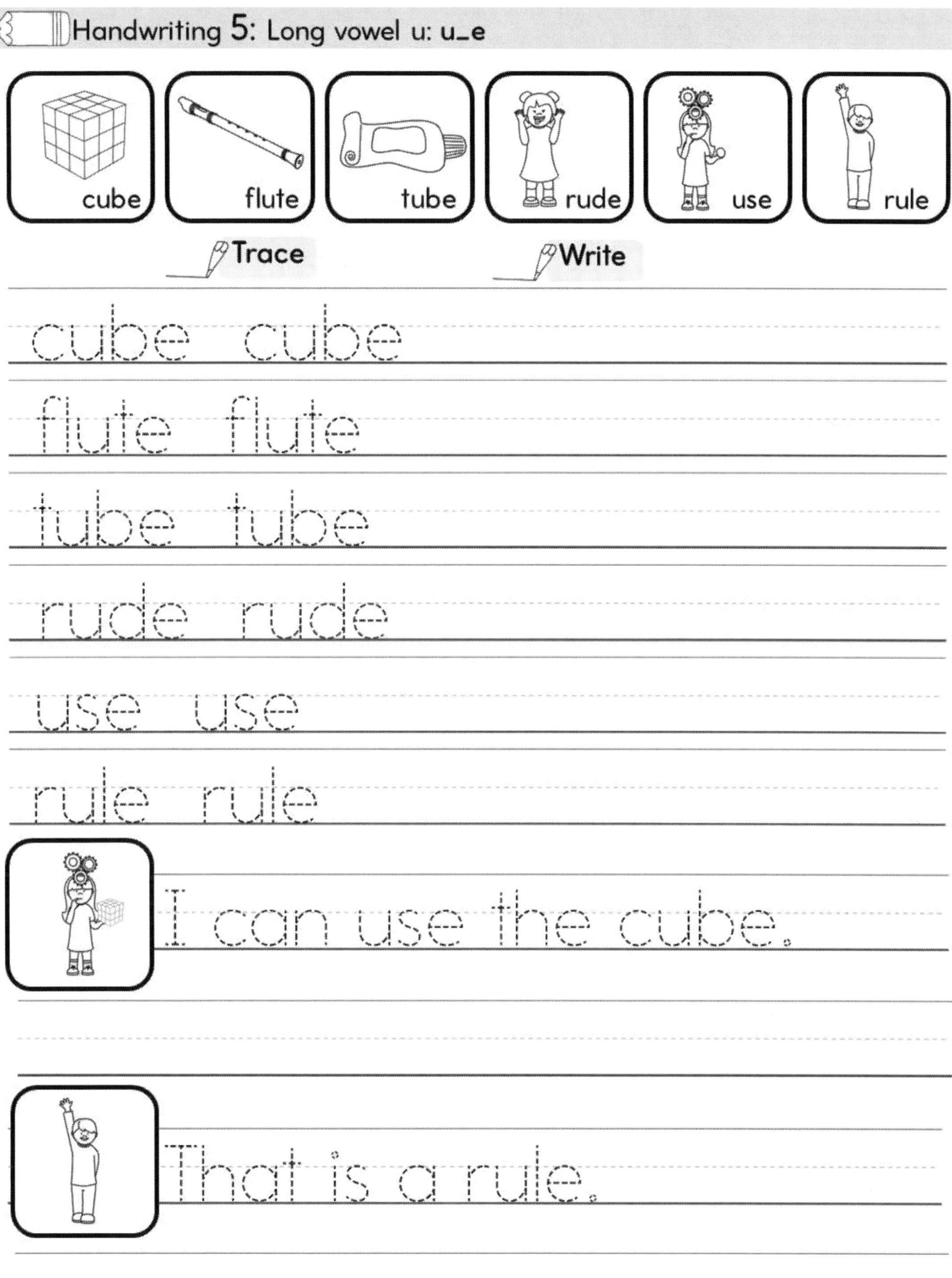

Phonics Lesson 5 Long vowel u: u_e

Middle Sounds Circle  the pictures that have the **long u** sound.

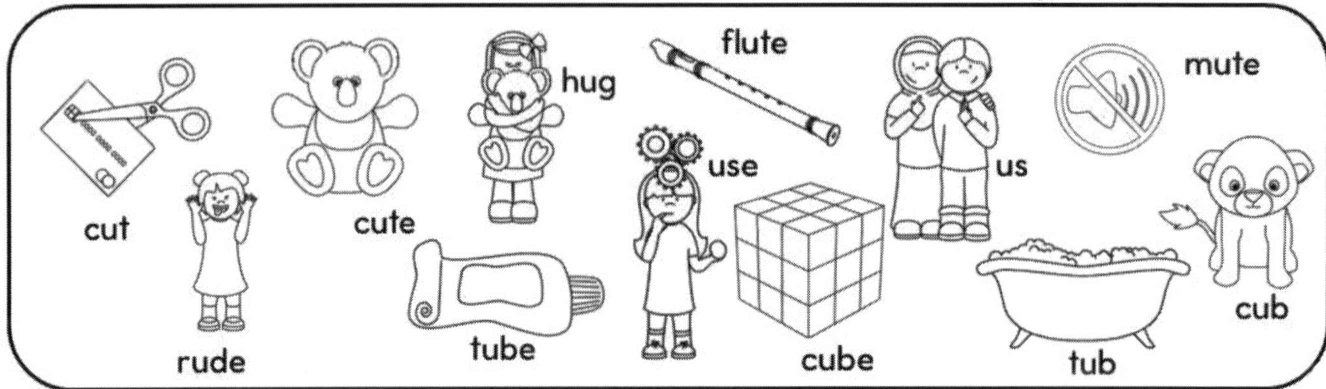

Read Words

us use cub cube cut cute

tub tube flute mute

hug dune

Read Sentences  Circle  the picture that matches the sentence.

I can use the cube to help.

Push on the tube to get the paste.

The cub is cute.

Spell Words

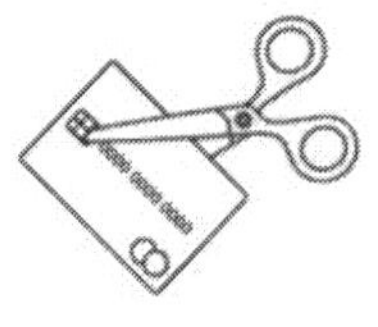

___ ___ ___

___ ___ ___ ___

___ ___ ___ ___

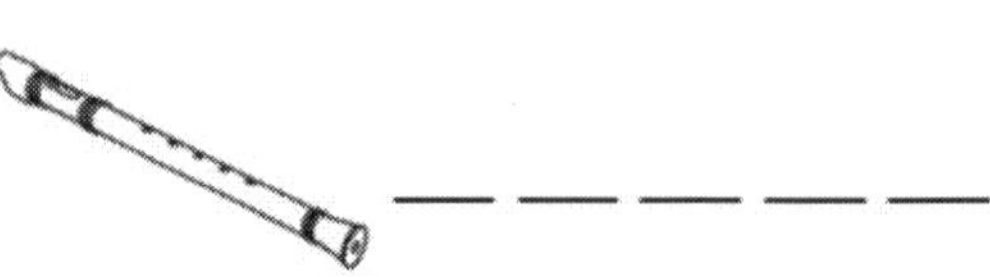

___ ___ ___ ___ ___

cut, cute, mute, flute

New Class

It is June. Luke is new to the Dune Class. The kids tell Luke the class rules. Put up a hand to talk. Do not be rude. Do not make excuses. The kids include Luke in the class games. The kids let Luke use the class cube. Luke can get a side of the cube red. Luke is glad he is in the Dune Class.

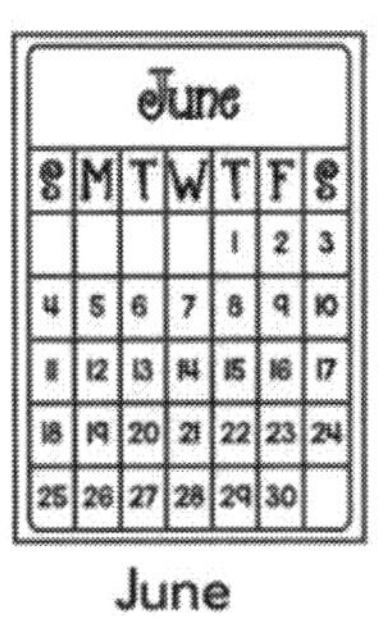

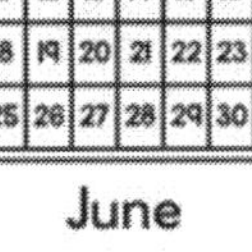
June

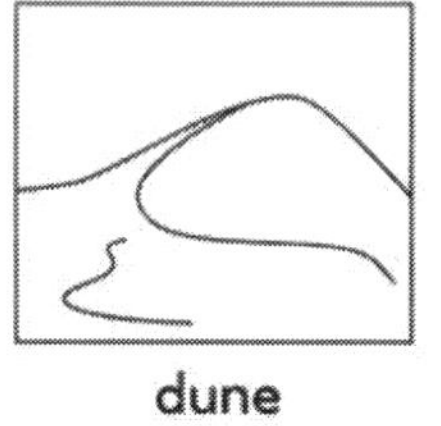
dune

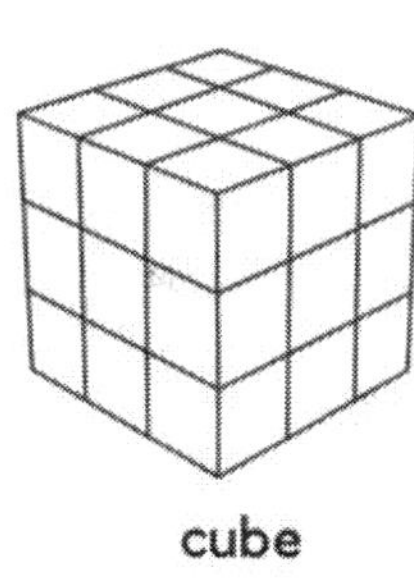
cube

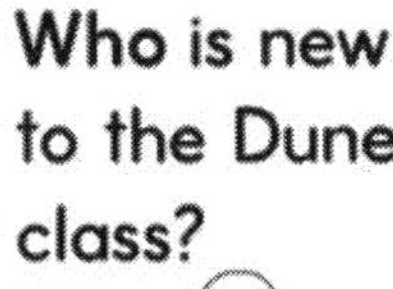
Who is new to the Dune class?

When does Luke come to the class?

What is a class rule?

What can Luke use?

Vocabulary 5: Long vowel u: u,_e

I can see the ___.	That is ____.	I can ____.
__ __ __ __	__ __ __ __	__ __ __ __
__ __ __ __ __	__ __ __ __	__ __ __
__ __ __ __	**Look at the ____.**	__ __ __ __ __
__ __ __ __	__ __ __ __	__ __ __ __ __ __ __
__ __ __ __	__ __ __ __ __	**It is ____.**
__ __ __ __ __	__ __ __ __ __ __ __	a __ __ __ __
		a __ __ __ __
		__ __ __ __ __ __
		__ __ __ __

Long Vowel e

e ee beet	e ee weed	e ee cheese
e ee tree	e ee street	e ee feed

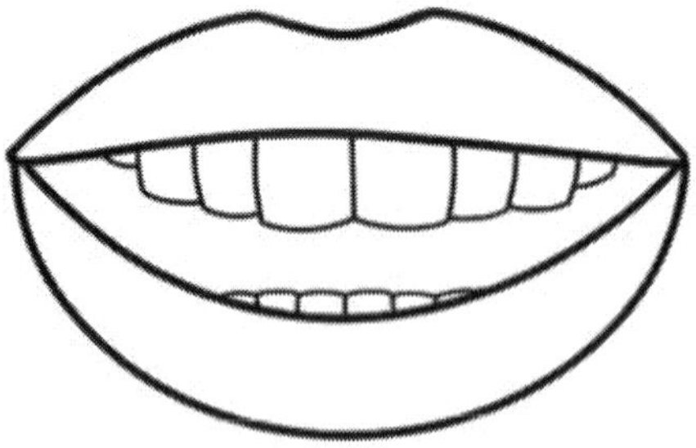

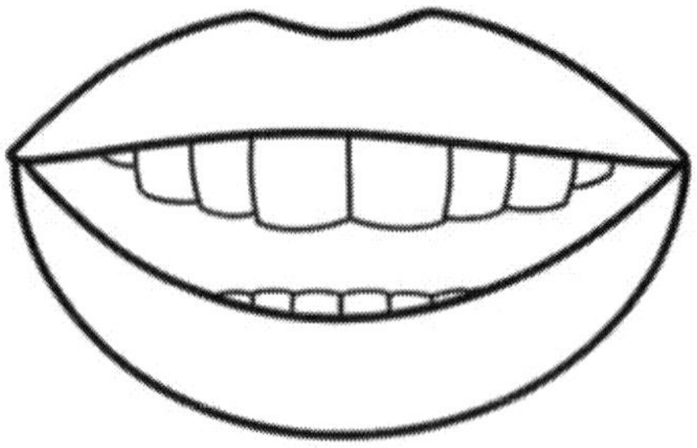

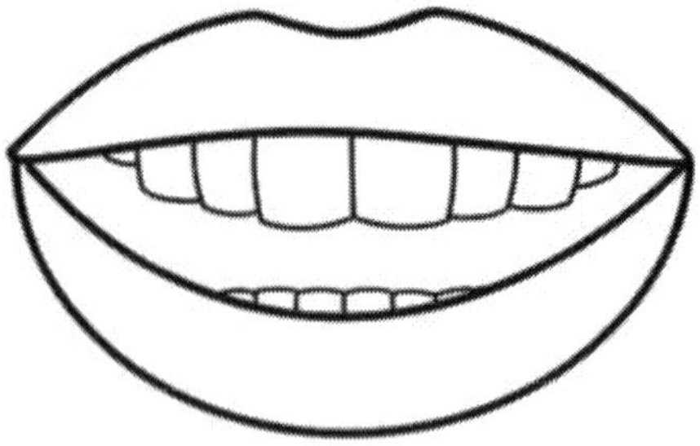

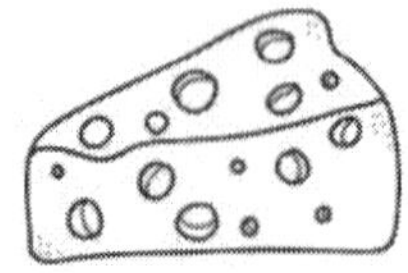

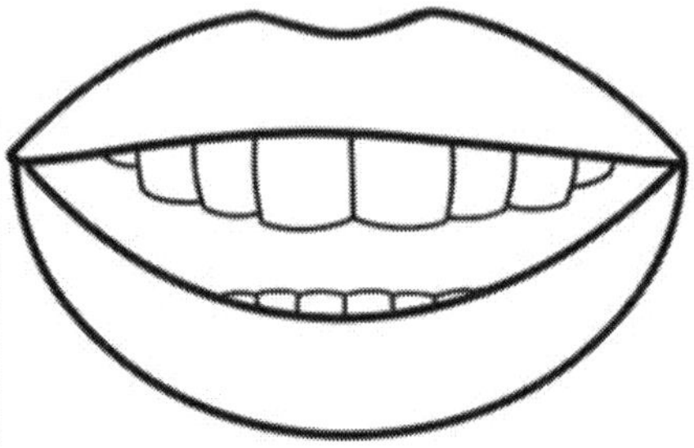

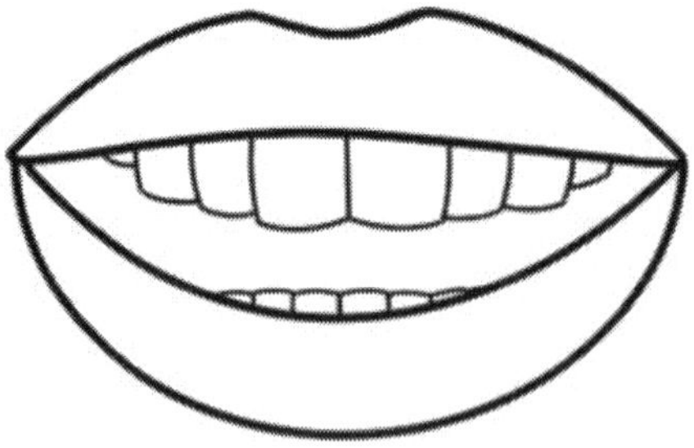

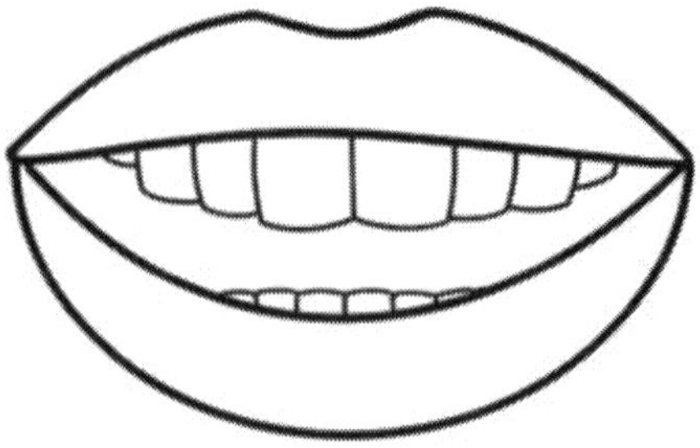

Handwriting 6: Long vowel e: **ee**

bee cheese feet tree need feed

Trace Write

bee bee

cheese cheese

feet feet

tree tree

need need

feed feed

A bee is in the tree.

I need a drink.

Phonics Lesson 6 Long vowel ee

Sounds Circle the letters that make the **long e** sound.

Read Words

see seed feed feet beet tree

green speed screen sweep weed

cheese bed meet pet wheel

Read Sentences Circle the picture that matches the sentence.

That is a green frog.

I see feet in the sand.

A bee is up in the tree.

____ _____ ______

____ ______ ____

see, tree, screen, feet, cheese, meet

The Weekend

It is the weekend. Bree must sweep up a mess. Lee feeds the dog. Bree and Lee peek into the kitchen and see Ben kneed. Bree and Lee get a snack. Bree gets cheese. Lee gets beets. Bree and Lee take the snack sit by a tree. Ben comes to the tree with coffee. Bree sits with her feet on the tree. Lee sits with her feet in the street. Ben sits with his feet in the weeds.

Who feeds the dog?

Where do Bree and Lee peek?

What does Lee have as a snack?

Where does Bree sit?

Vocabulary 6: Long vowel e: ee

I can see the ___.	I see ___.	I can ___.
bee	green	feed
beet	greed	sweep
knee	three	meet
cheese	**That is ___.**	peek
seed	steep	kneed
screen	**It can ___.**	sleep
feet	speed	sneeze*
beef	see	**I need water.**
sheep	freeze*	need
steel	squeeze*	*English words do not end with z.
heel	**Go to the ___.**	
peel	weed	
coffee	tree	
	wheel	
	street	

Vocabulary and Spelling 6: Long vowel e: ee

I can see the ___.	I see _____.	I can _____.
___ ___ ___	___ ___ ___ ___ ___	___ ___ ___ ___
___ ___ ___ ___	___ ___ ___ ___ ___	___ ___ ___ ___ ___
___ ___ ___ ___	___ ___ ___ ___ ___	___ ___ ___ ___
___ ___ ___ ___ ___ ___	**That is _____.**	___ ___ ___ ___
___ ___ ___ ___	___ ___ ___ ___ ___	___ ___ ___ ___ ___
___ ___ ___ ___ ___ ___	**It can _____.**	___ ___ ___ ___ ___
___ ___ ___ ___	___ ___ ___ ___ ___	___ ___ ___ ___ ___ ___ *
___ ___ ___ ___	___ ___ ___	**I need water.**
___ ___ ___ ___ ___	___ ___ ___ ___ ___ ___ *	___ ___ ___ ___
___ ___ ___ ___ ___	___ ___ ___ ___ ___ ___ ___ *	*English words do not end with z.
___ ___ ___ ___	**Go to the _____.**	
___ ___ ___ ___	___ ___ ___ ___	
___ ___ ___ ___ ___ ___	___ ___ ___ ___	
	___ ___ ___ ___ ___	
	___ ___ ___ ___ ___	

Long Vowel e

e ea eat	e ea team	e ea peach
e ea leaf	e ea seal	e ea teach

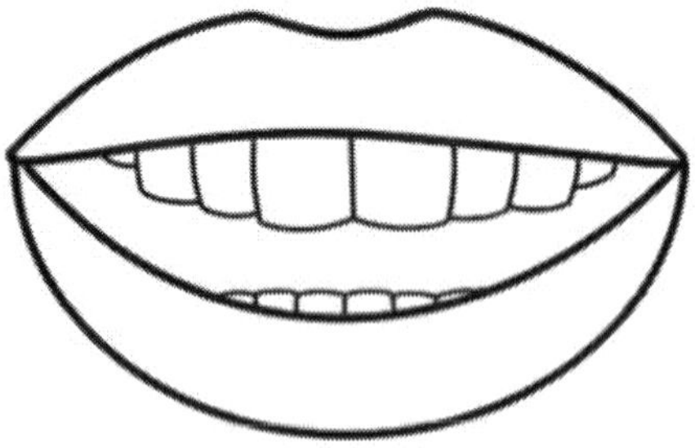

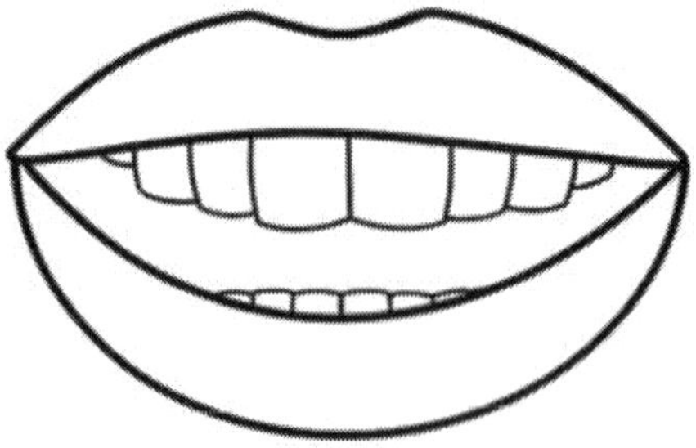

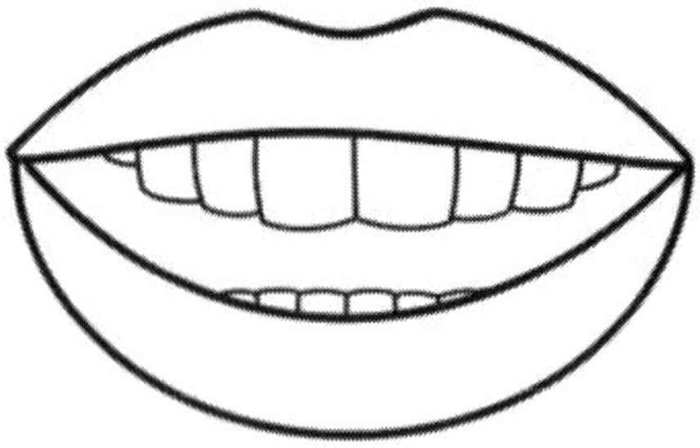

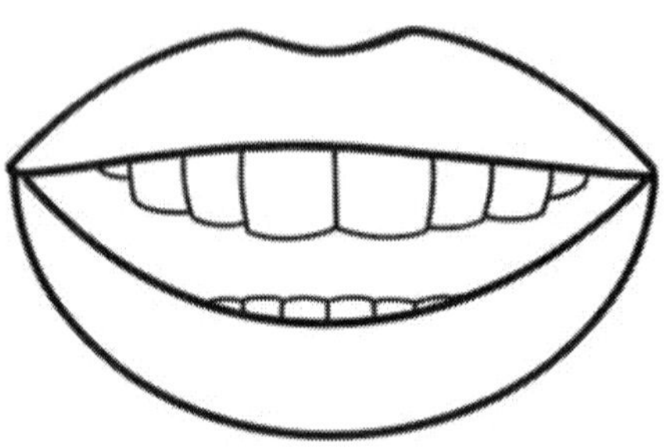

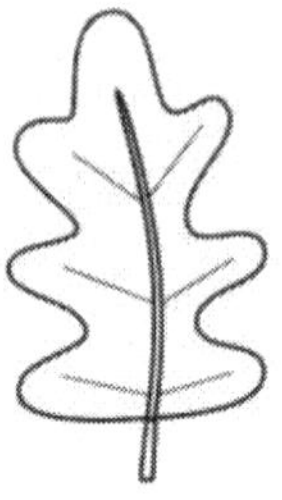

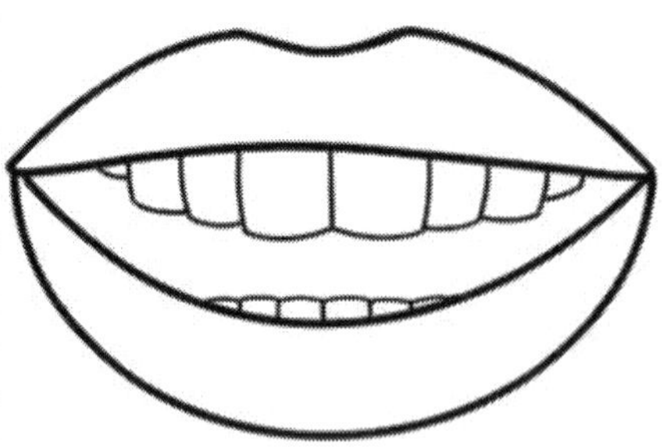

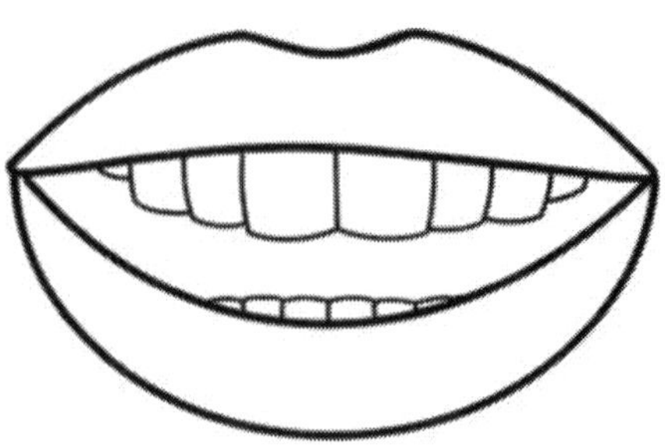

peach tea team meal read eat

Trace Write

peach peach

tea tea

team team

meal meal

read read

eat eat

I can eat a peach.

I will eat a meal.

Phonics Lesson 7 Long vowel ea

Sounds Circle the letters that make the **long e** sound.

Read Words

eat meat sea tea team dream
beach reach see leak tree
clean shelf bead seal pet

Read Sentences  Circle  the picture that matches the sentence.

I can reach the beads.

The bucket has a big leak.

You must not cheat on a test.

 _ _ _

_ _ _ _ _

 _ _ _ _ _

_ _ _ _ _

 _ _ _ _ _

 _ _ _ _

Baseball

Ren will lead the red team. The kids must not tease or cheat on the team. That is mean. Ren yells go, go, go when the red team runs. Ren helps the red team hush when a kid is at bat. Ren and the team scream YES when a red kid runs to home base. Ren helps teach a new kit to hit. At the end of the game the team eats a meal.

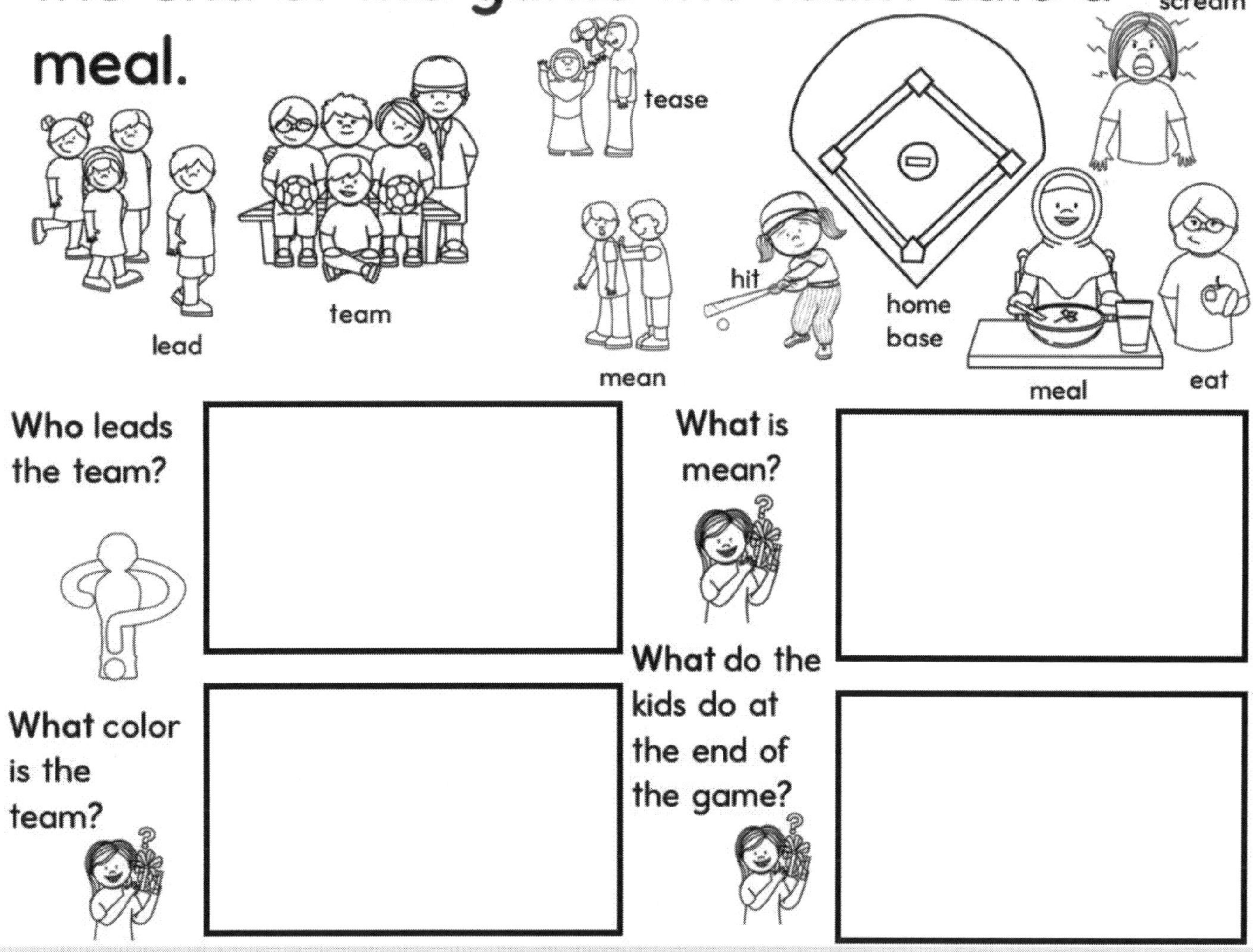

Who leads the team?

What is mean?

What color is the team?

What do the kids do at the end of the game?

Vocabulary 7: Long vowel 3: ea

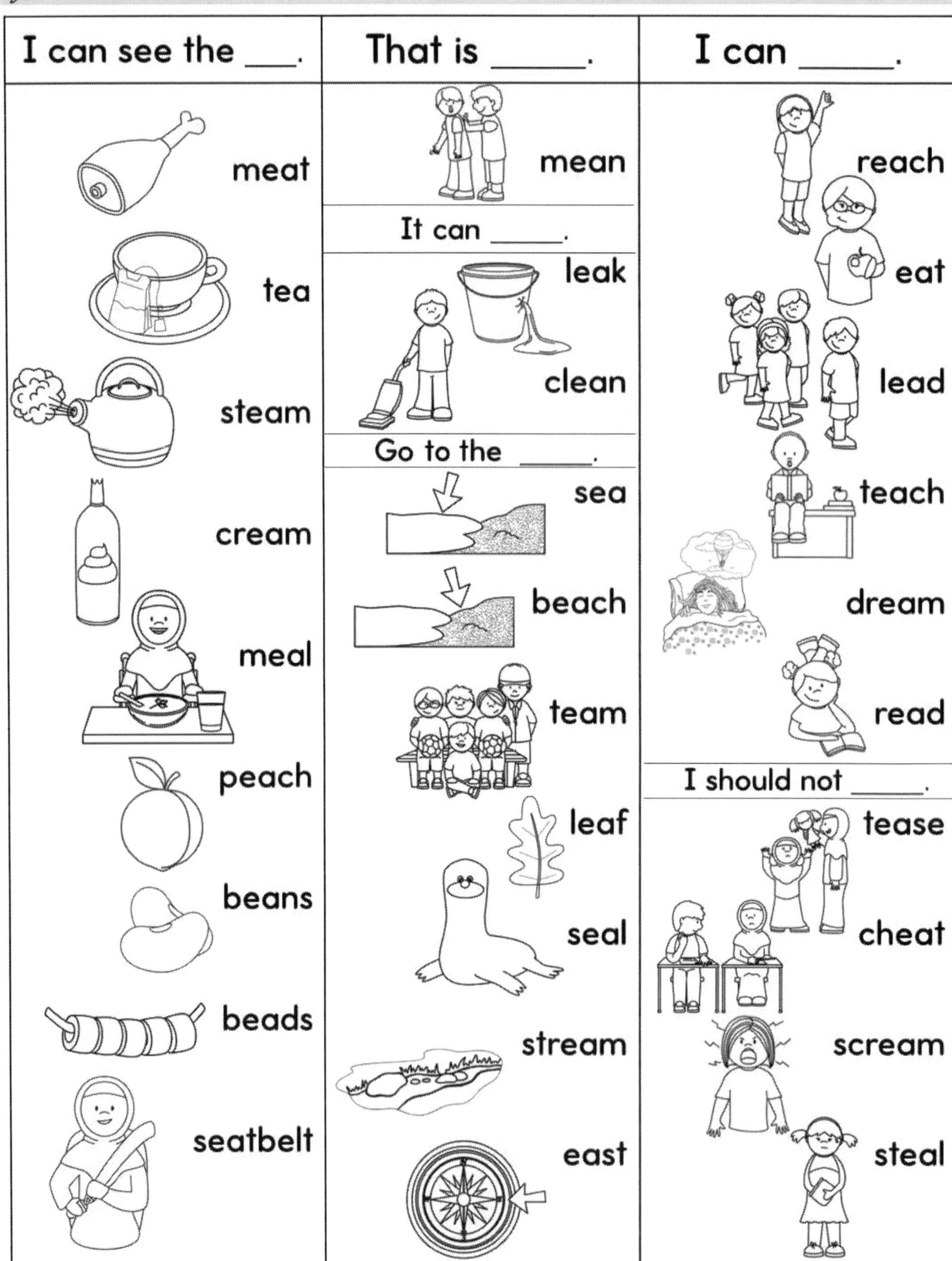

I can see the ___.	That is _____.	I can _____.
_ _ _ _	_ _ _ _	_ _ _ _ _
_ _ _	**It can _____.**	_ _ _
_ _ _ _ _	_ _ _ _	_ _ _ _
_ _ _ _ _	_ _ _ _ _	_ _ _ _ _
_ _ _ _	**Go to the _____.**	_ _ _ _ _
_ _ _ _ _	_ _ _	_ _ _ _
_ _ _ _ _	_ _ _ _ _	**I should not _____.**
_ _ _ _ _	_ _ _ _	_ _ _ _ _
_ _ _ _ _ _ _	_ _ _ _	_ _ _ _ _
	_ _ _ _	_ _ _ _ _
	_ _ _ _ _ _	_ _ _ _ _
	_ _ _ _	

Long Vowel a

a ay clay	a ai chain	a ai pail
a ay hay	a ai paint	a ai snail

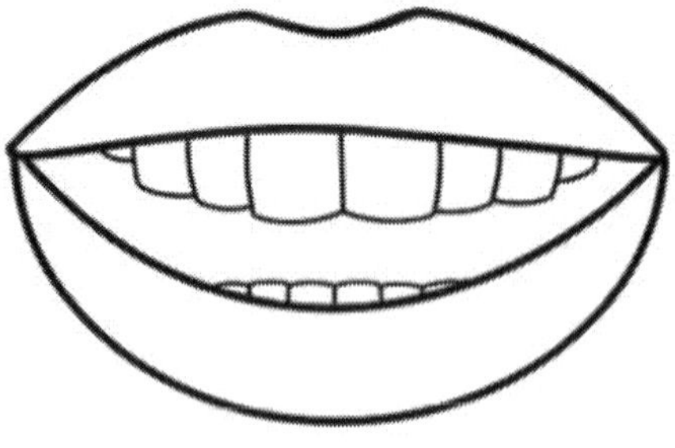

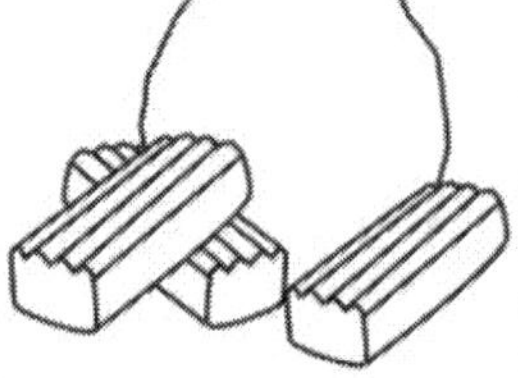

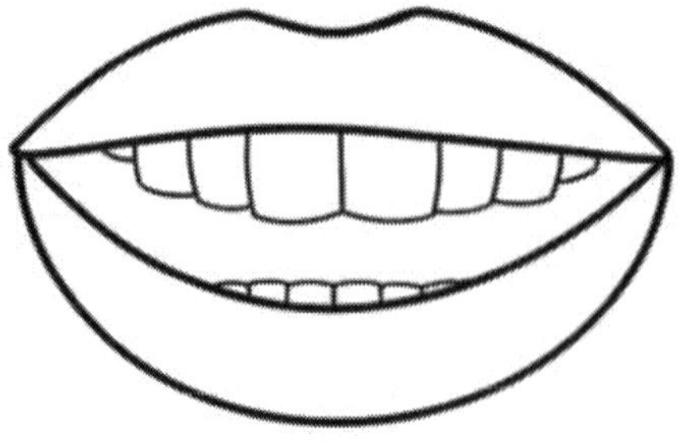

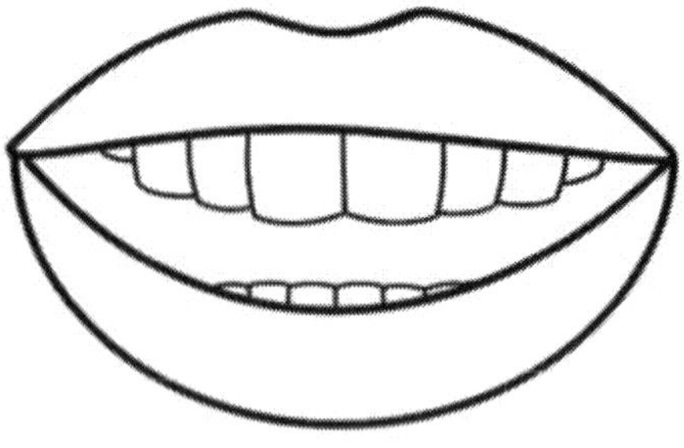

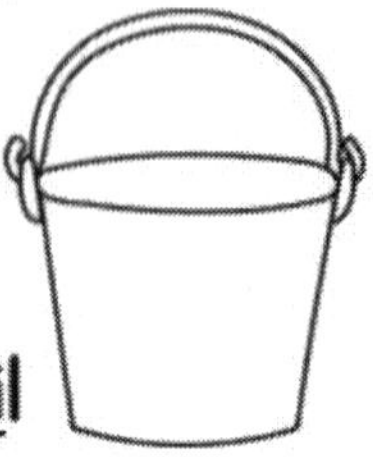

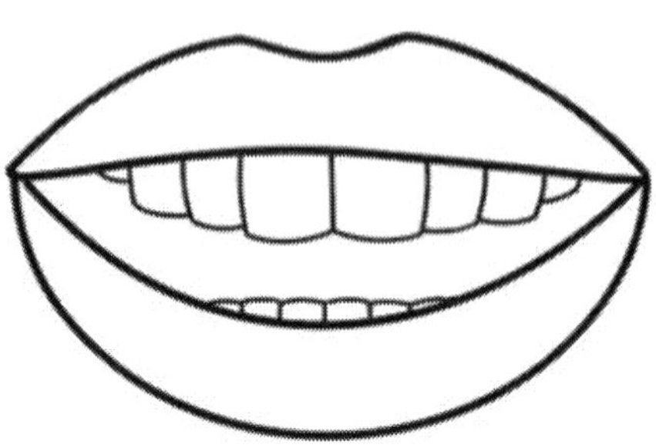

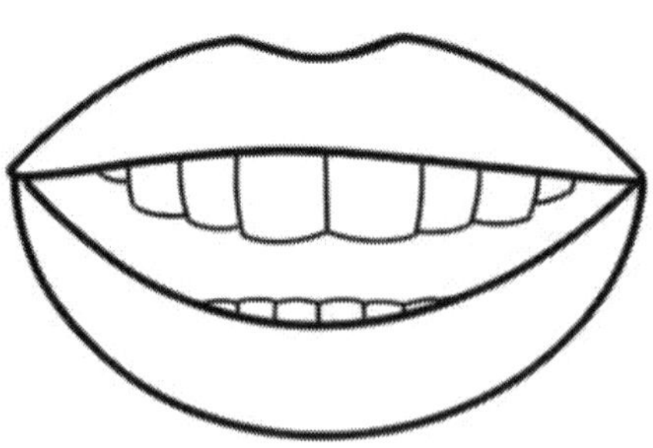

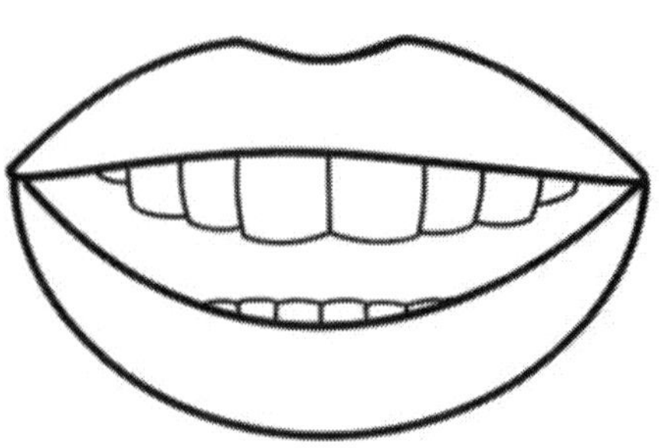

Handwriting 8: Long vowel a: ay, ai

train chain clay rain paint play

Trace Write

train train

chain chain

clay clay

rain rain

paint paint

play play

I can paint the rain.

I play a game.

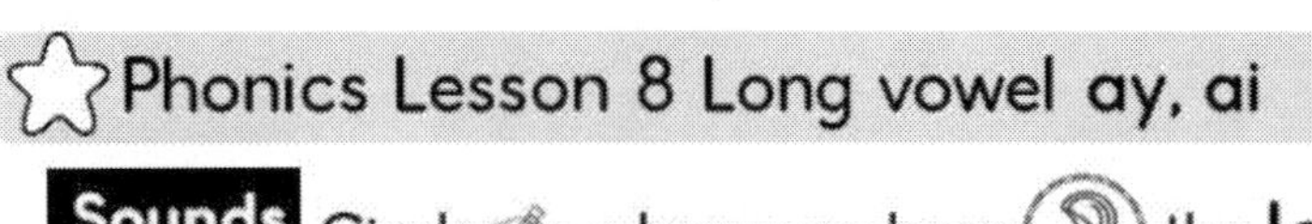

Phonics Lesson 8 Long vowel ay, ai

Sounds Circle where you hear the **long a** sound.

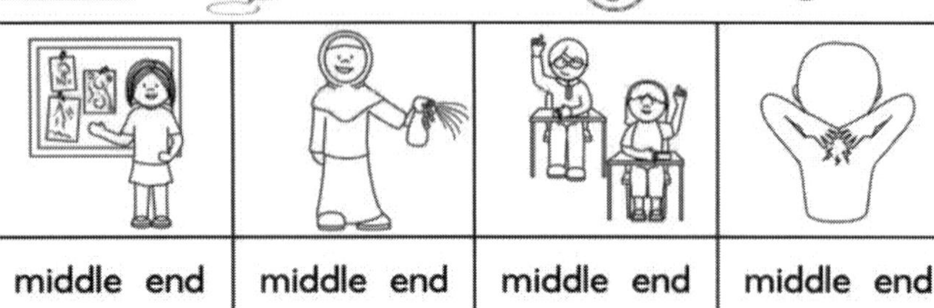

middle end	middle end	middle end	middle end

Ending Sounds

Circle the pictures where you hear the **long a** sound at the end.

Read Words

pay stay play lay
paint wait braid
brain tray train
*mail snail nail

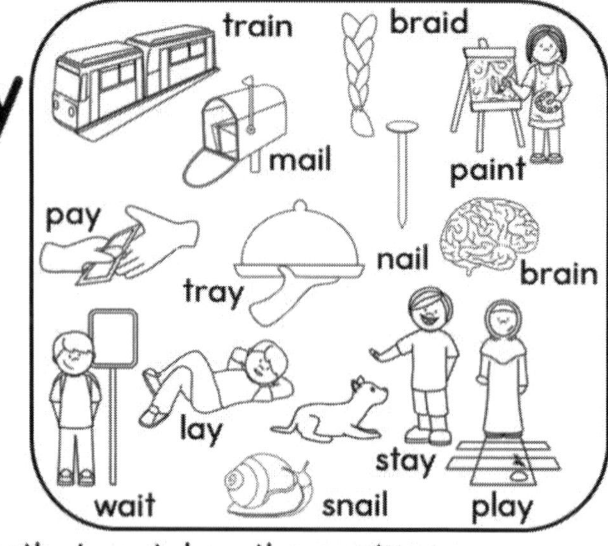

Read Sentences Circle the picture that matches the sentence.

It is fun to play in the rain.
I must wait to get on the train.

Tell the dog to stay.

Spell Words

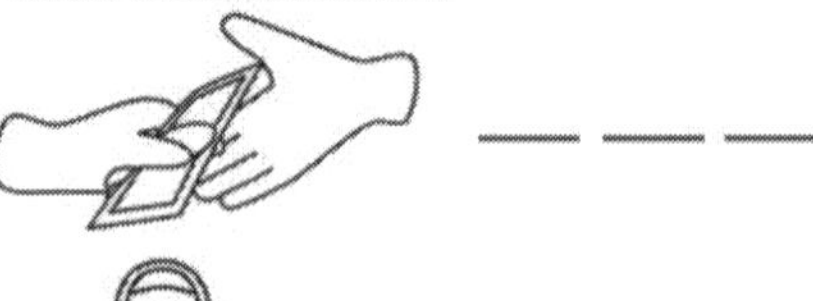 ___ ___ ___

___ ___ ___ ___ ___

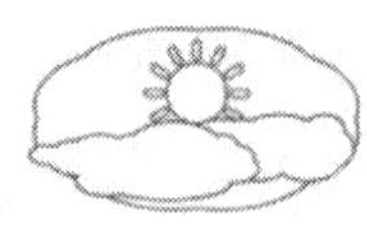 ___ ___ ___

 ___ ___ ___ ___

 ___ ___ ___ ___ ___

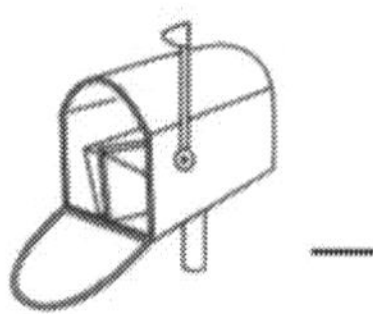 ___ ___ ___ ___

The Day

Ray must wait for her train. The train takes Ray to a spot to make crafts. Ray spray paints a display. Pam makes a clay snail.

Ray spots Pam. Ray and Pam make a plan. The next day Ray and Pam hike on a trail. The kids see a chain. Past the chain is hay. Pam lays on top of the hay. Then the kids play on the hay. It is a fun day.

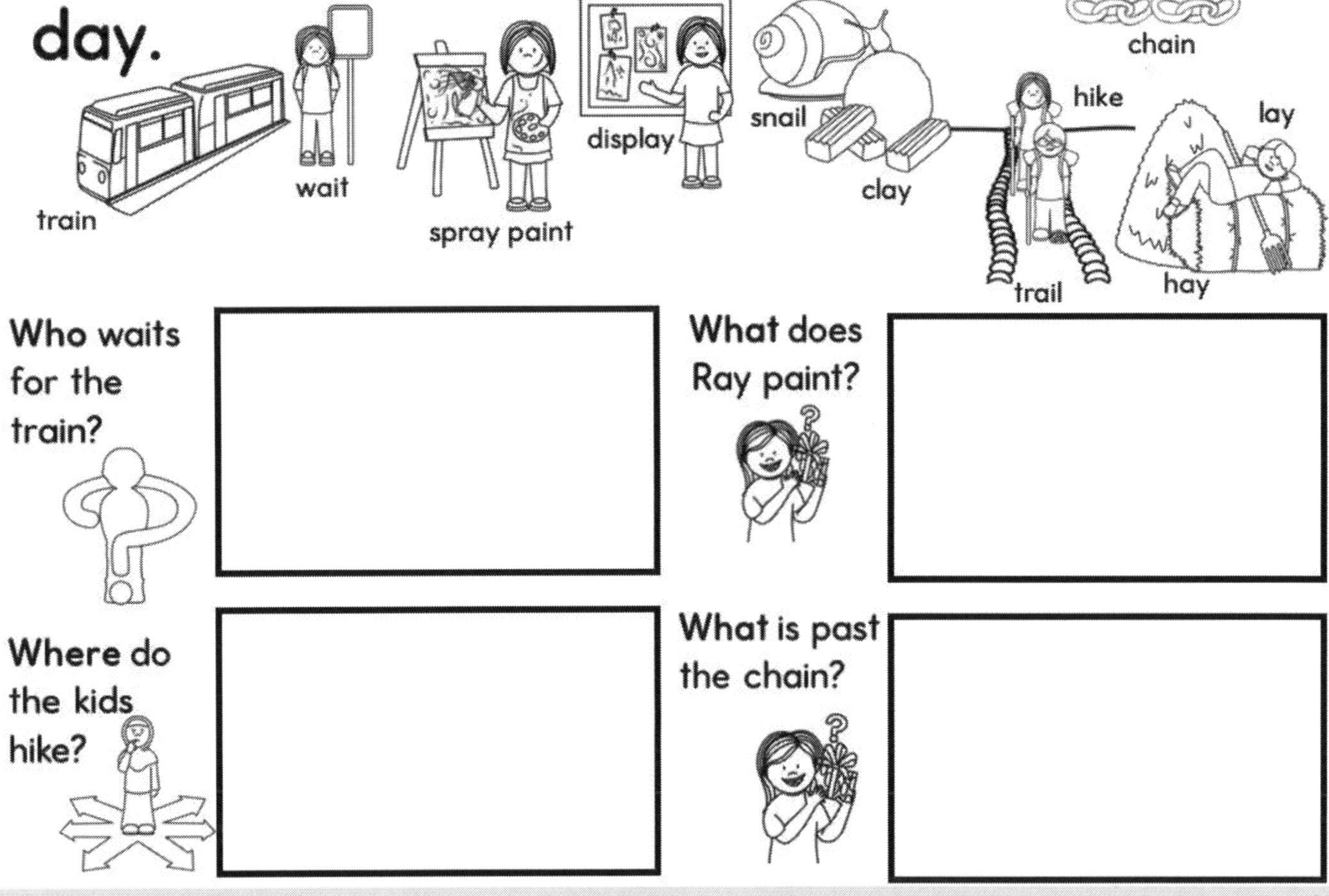

Who waits for the train?

What does Ray paint?

Where do the kids hike?

What is past the chain?

I see a _____.	That is _____.	I can _____.
braid	a waist	aim
train	a display	wait
brain	a trail	faint
chain	mail	paint
drain	clay	raise
pail	hay	spray
snail	**It is _____.** day	play
nail	**It can _____.** rain	pay
tray	stay	lay
I have a _____. pain	**Which way?** way	say

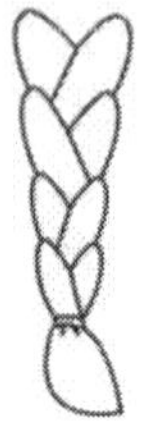

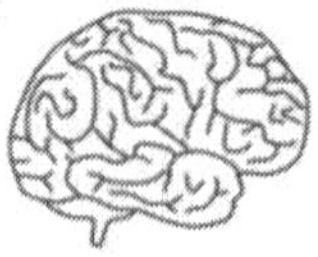

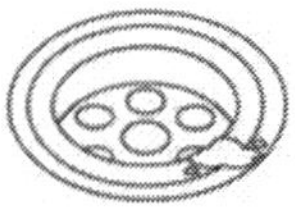

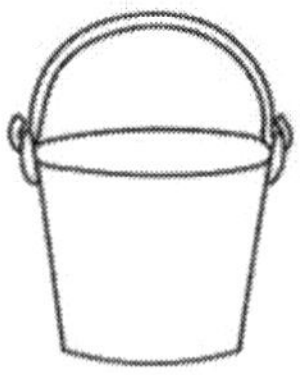

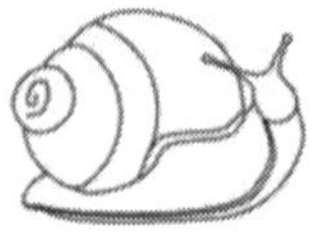

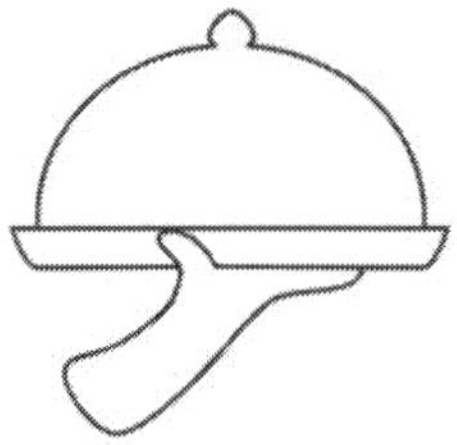

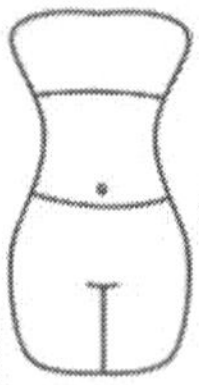

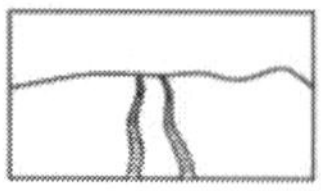

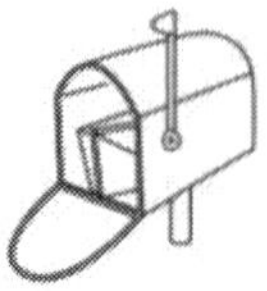

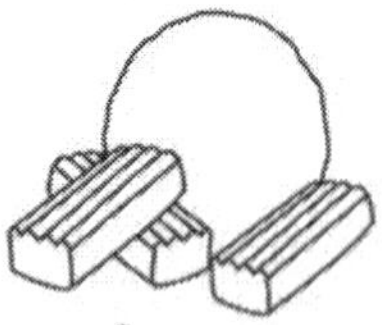

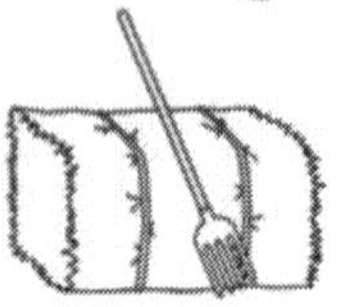

Vocabulary and Spelling 8: Long vowel a: ai, ay

I see a _____.	That is _____.	I can _____.
_ _ _ _ _	a _ _ _ _ _	_ _ _
_ _ _ _ _	a _ _ _ _ _ _	_ _ _ _
_ _ _ _ _	a _ _ _ _ _	_ _ _ _ _
_ _ _ _ _	_ _ _ _	_ _ _ _ _
_ _ _ _ _	_ _ _ _	_ _ _ _ _
_ _ _ _	_ _ _	_ _ _ _ _
_ _ _ _ _	**It is _____.**	_ _ _ _
_ _ _ _	_ _ _	_ _ _
_ _ _ _	**It can _____.**	_ _ _
I have a _____.	_ _ _ _	_ _ _
_ _ _ _	_ _ _ _	
	Which way?	
	_ _ _	

Long Vowel o

o oa goat	o oa coach	o oa float
o ow snow	o ow row	o ow bowl

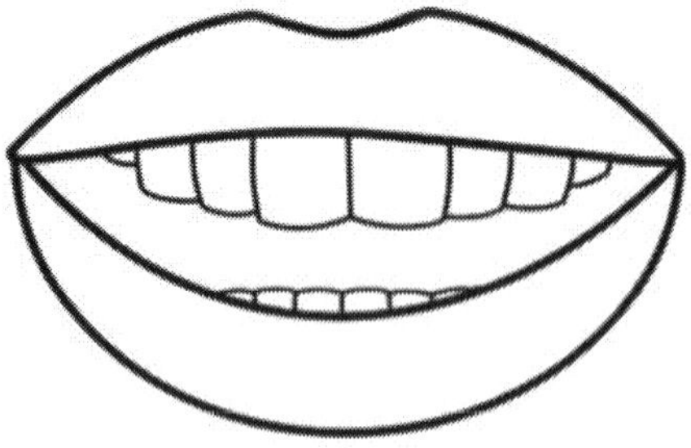

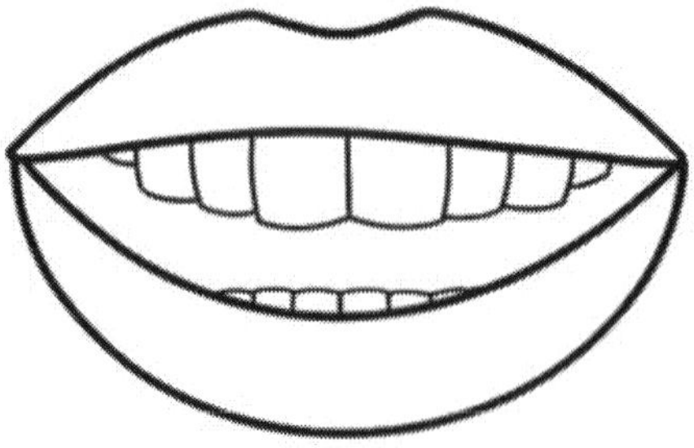

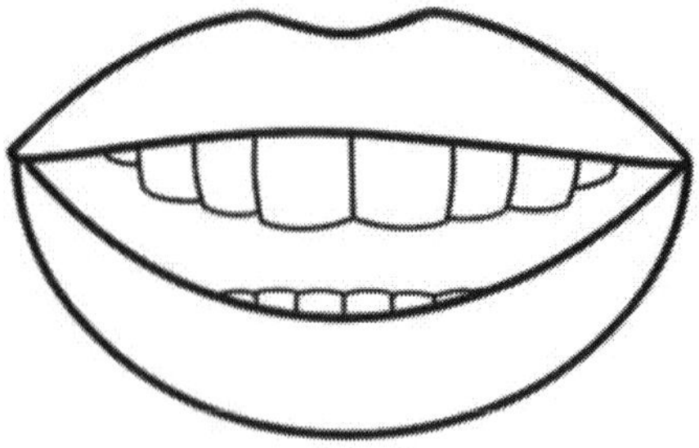

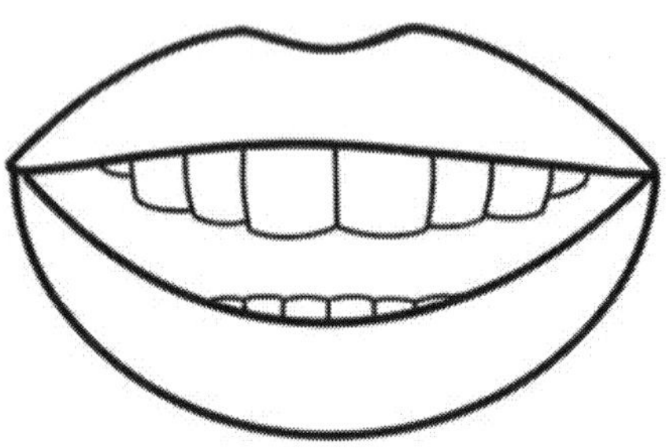

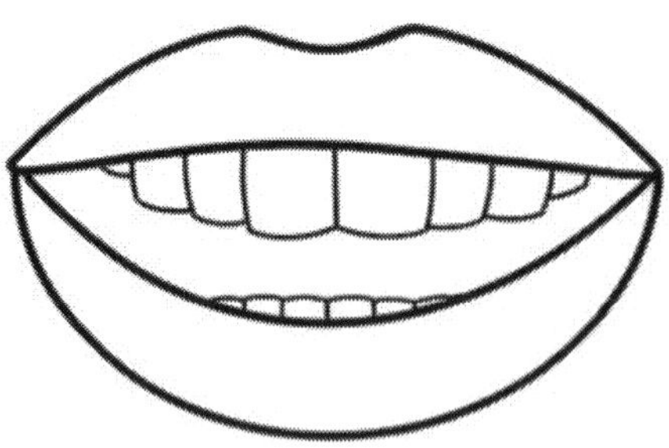

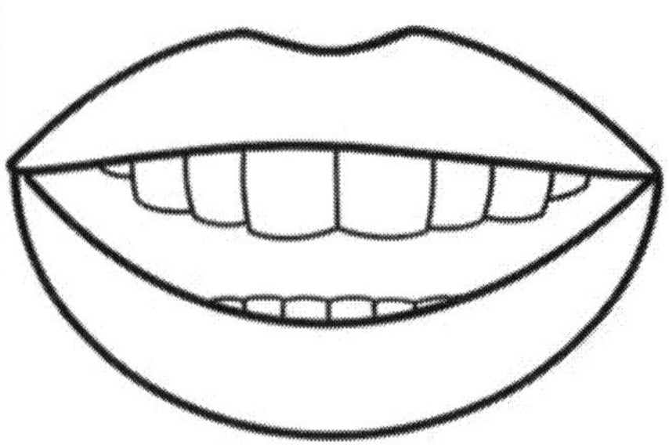

Handwriting 9: Long vowel o: oa, ow

snow road soap bowl coat throat

Trace Write

snow snow

road road

soap soap

bowl bowl

coat coat

throat throat

Snow is on the road.

He put on a coat.

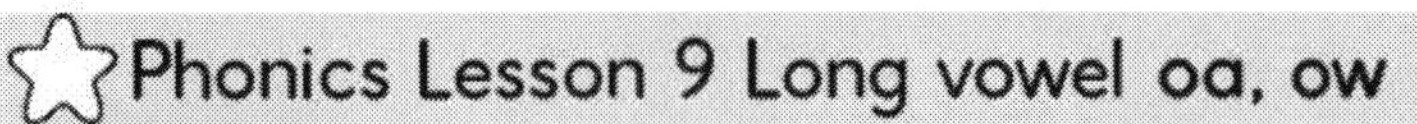

Phonics Lesson 9 Long vowel oa, ow

Sounds Circle where you hear 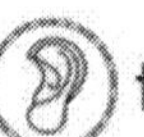 the **long o** sound.

	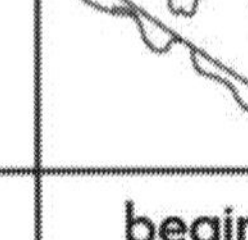		
beginning middle end	beginning middle end	beginning middle end	beginning middle end

Ending Sounds

Circle the pictures where you hear  the **long o** sound at the end.

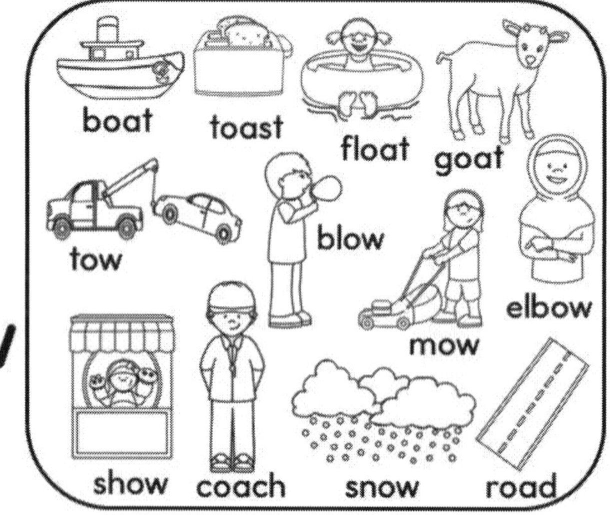

Read Words

boat goat toast
tow mow snow
coach road elbow
float blow show

Read Sentences Circle  the picture that matches the sentence.

I must mow the grass.
The tow truck is on the road.
That goat is in the snow.

Spell Words

 _ _ _ _  _ _ _ _ 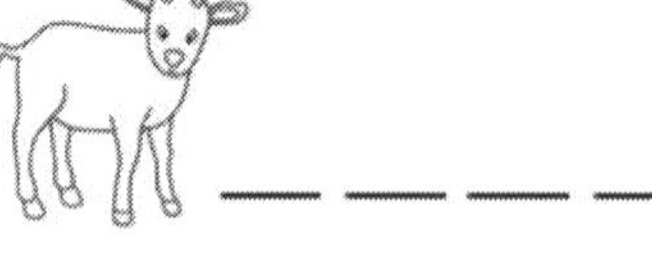 _ _ _ _

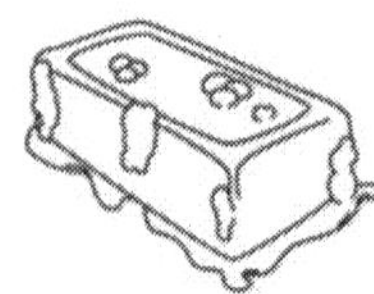

 _ _ _ _ _  _ _ _ _  _ _ _ _ _

Camp

The kids go to camp. Sam floats on the lake. Pam rows a boat. The coach shows the kids how to aim a bow and arrow. Do not hit the oak tree! Down the road the kids can see a goat, a sheep, and a tree frog. The goat and the sheep drink out of a bowl. One day it snows. The camp is closed.

Vocabulary 9: Long vowel o: oa, ow

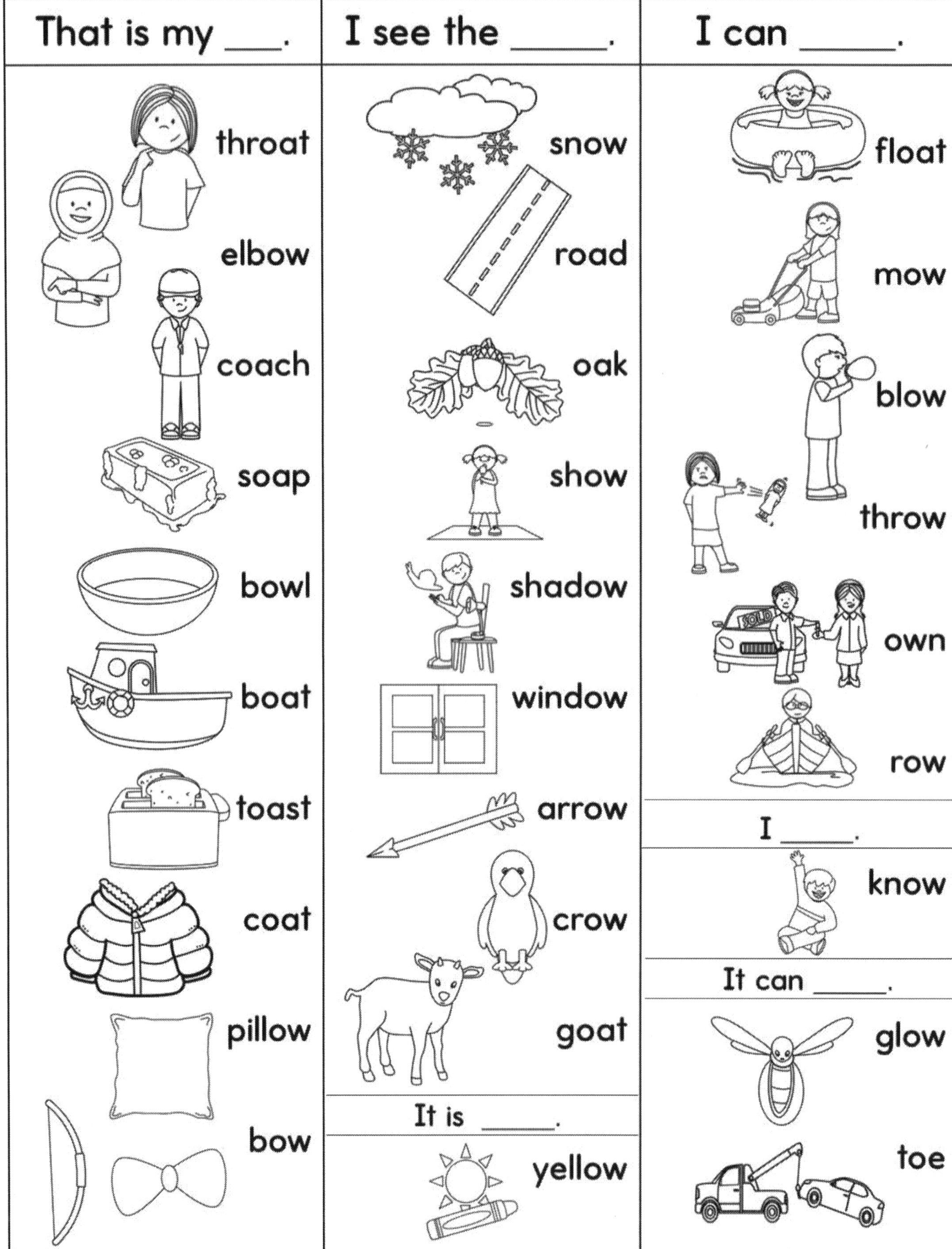

That is my ___.	I see the _____.	I can _____.
_ _ _ _ _ _	_ _ _ _	_ _ _ _ _
_ _ _ _ _	_ _ _ _	_ _ _
_ _ _ _ _	_ _ _	_ _ _ _
_ _ _ _ _	_ _ _ _	_ _ _ _ _
_ _ _ _	_ _ _ _ _ _	_ _ _
_ _ _ _	_ _ _ _ _ _	_ _ _
_ _ _ _ _	_ _ _ _ _	I _____.
_ _ _ _	_ _ _ _	_ _ _ _
_ _ _ _ _ _	_ _ _ _	It can _____.
_ _ _	It is _____.	_ _ _ _
	_ _ _ _ _ _	_ _ _

Long Vowel i

i igh light	i y fly	i ie pie
i igh night	i y my	i ie tie

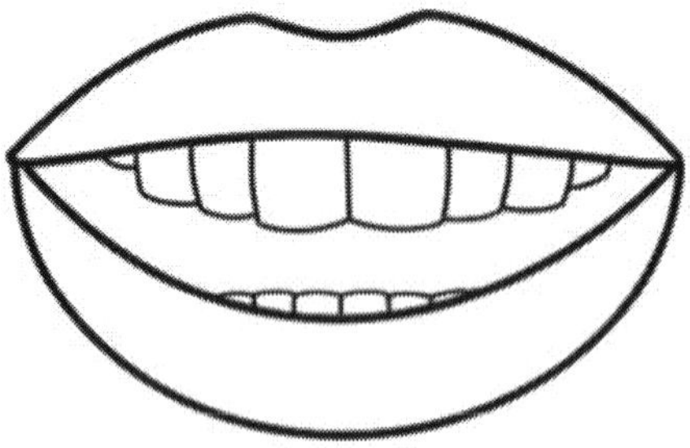

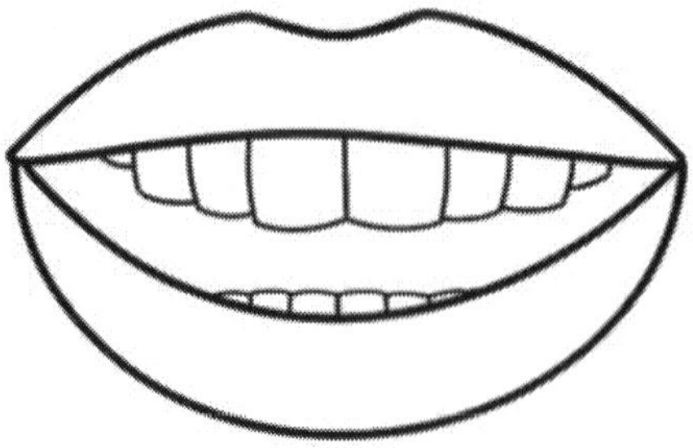

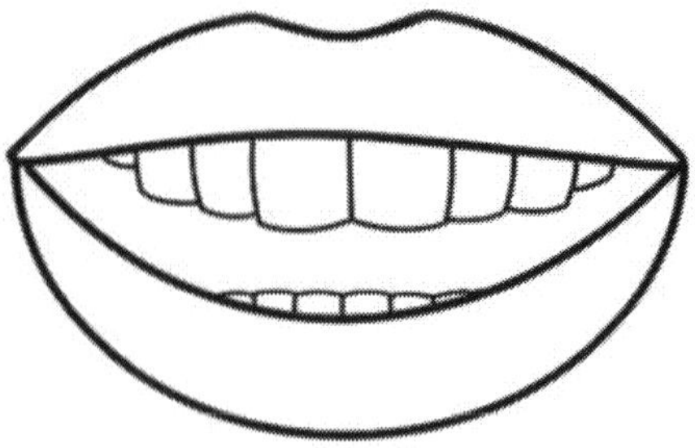

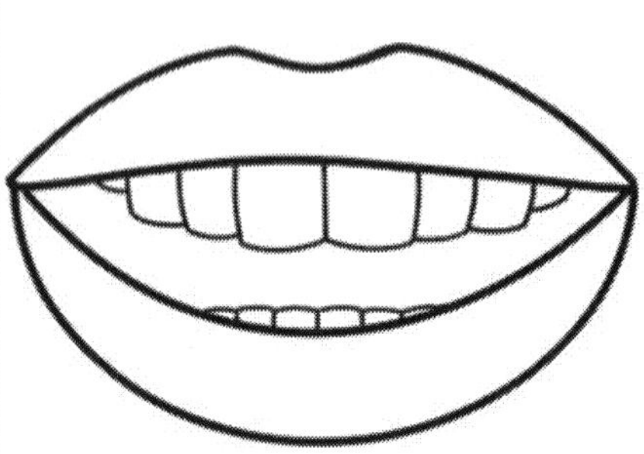

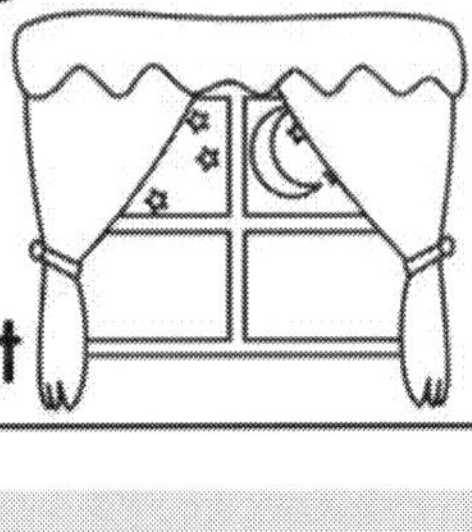

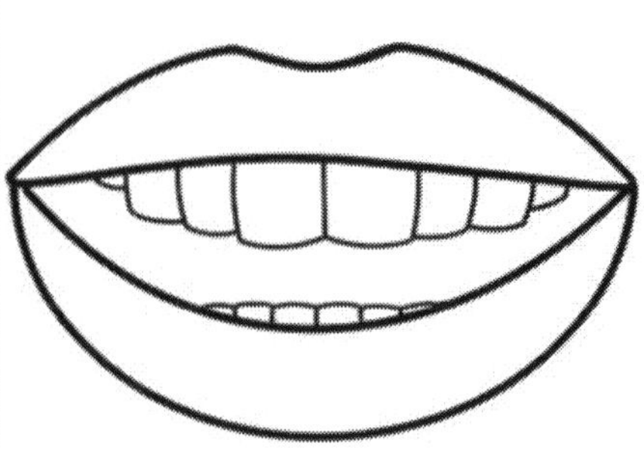

Handwriting 10: Long vowel i: igh, y, ie

light night why fly my tie

Trace Write

light light

night night

why why

fly fly

my my

tie tie

Why can that fly?

The light is bright.

Phonics Lesson 10 Long vowel igh, y, ie

Sounds Circle where you hear the **long i** sound.

middle end	middle end	middle end	middle end

Ending Sounds

Circle the pictures where you hear the **long i** sound at the end.

Read Words

night light bright
buy fly sky try dry
fight tight pie tie

Read Sentences Circle the picture that matches the sentence.

The light is bright.

The kids got in a big fight.

I can dry my hands.

Spell Words

__ __

__ __ __ __ __

__ __ __

__ __ __

__ __ __ __ __

__ __ __ __ __

my, night, dry, buy, light, tight

The Babysitter

Milo has a job. He helps with Pip. Pip is not shy of Milo. Milo gets a fly out of the crib. He stops the bright light. He puts Pip into the crib to sleep. At midnight Pip gets up. The sky is dark. What will Milo try? Milo picks Pip up high. Milo puts Pip back into the crib. No luck. Milo gets Pip pie. Pip does not cry. Pip eats the pip. Then Pip goes back to sleep. Pie was just right for Pip.

Vocabulary 10: Long vowel i: igh, y, ie

I see (a, the) ____.	That is ____.	I can ______.
light	tight	dry
night	bright	buy
sky	my	try
fly	high	fry
thigh	right	fight
pie	**It is ____.**	**Go to the ____.**
tie	midnight	right
why	**I am____.**	**It can ____.**
	shy	cry
		fly

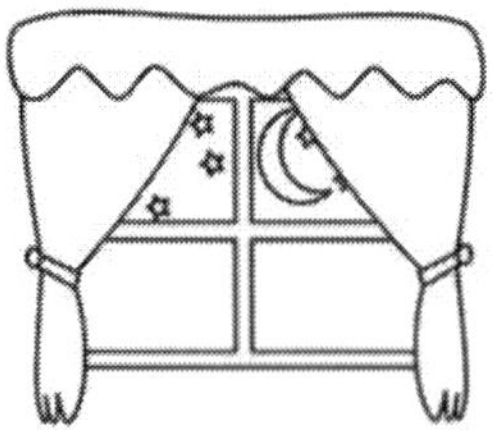

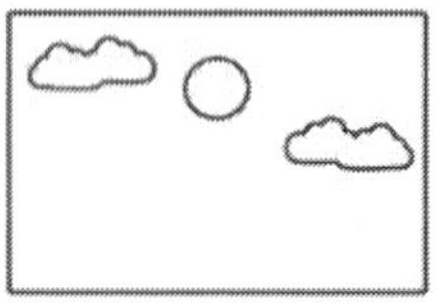

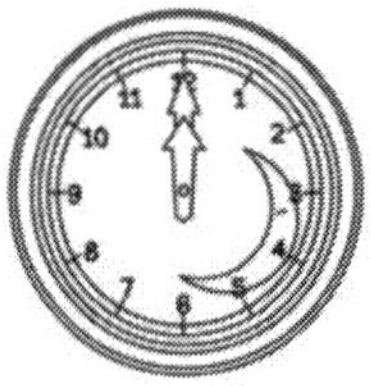

I see (a, the) ___.	That is ___.	I can ___.
_ _ _ _ _	_ _ _ _ _	_ _ _
_ _ _ _ _	_ _ _ _ _ _	_ _ _
_ _ _	_ _	_ _ _
_ _ _	_ _ _ _	_ _ _
_ _ _ _ _	_ _ _ _ _	_ _ _ _ _
_ _ _	**It is ___.**	**Go to the ___.**
_ _ _	_ _ _ _ _ _ _ _	_ _ _ _ _
_ _ _	**I am___.**	**It can ___.**
	_ _ _	_ _ _
		_ _ _

Long Vowel u

u ew stew	u ui fruit	u ue glue
u ew new	u ui suit	u ue fuel

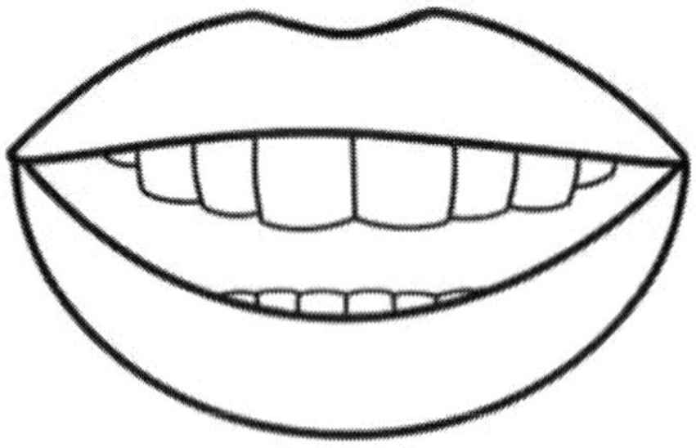

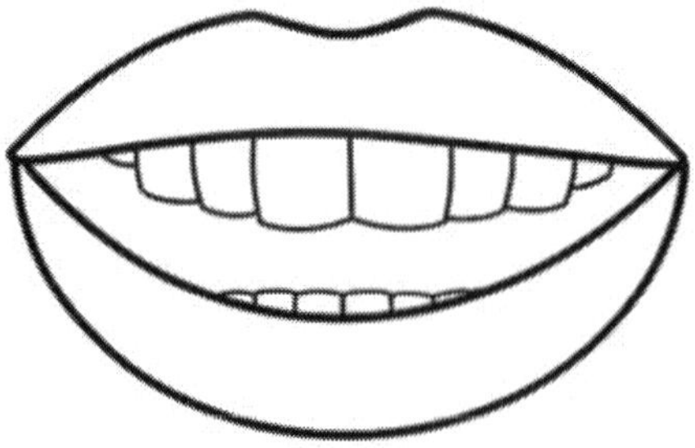

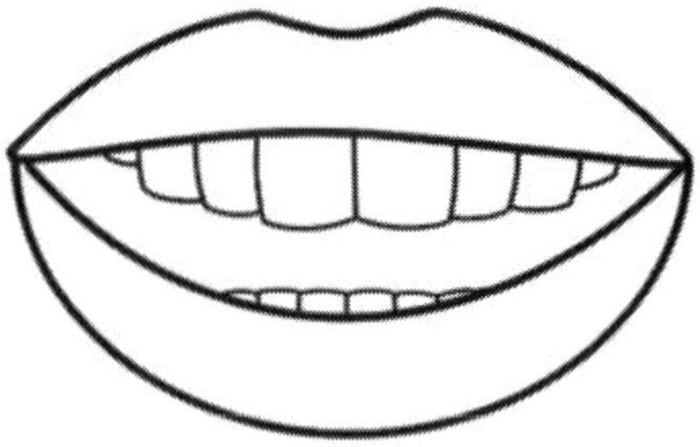

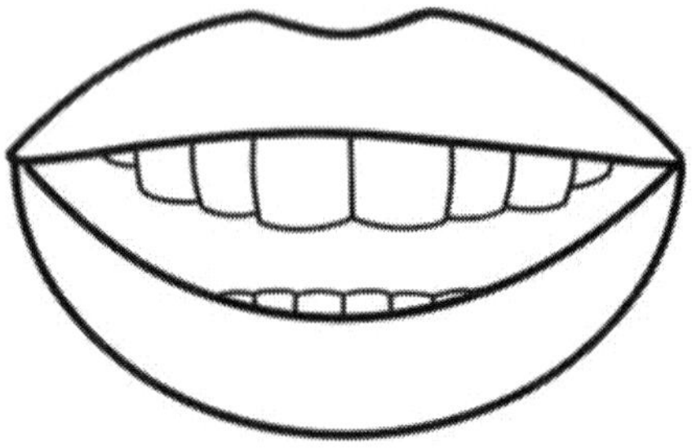

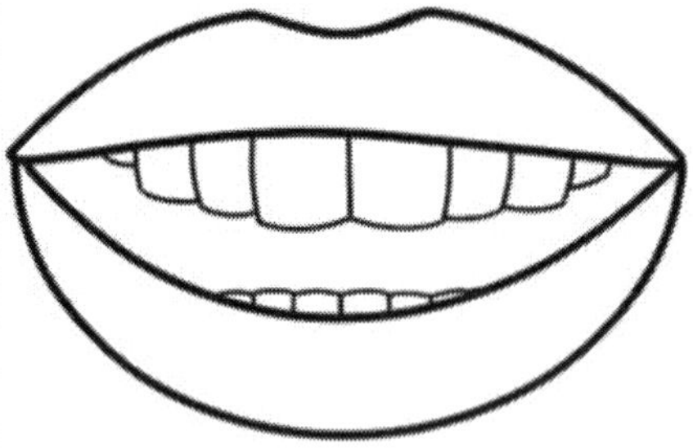

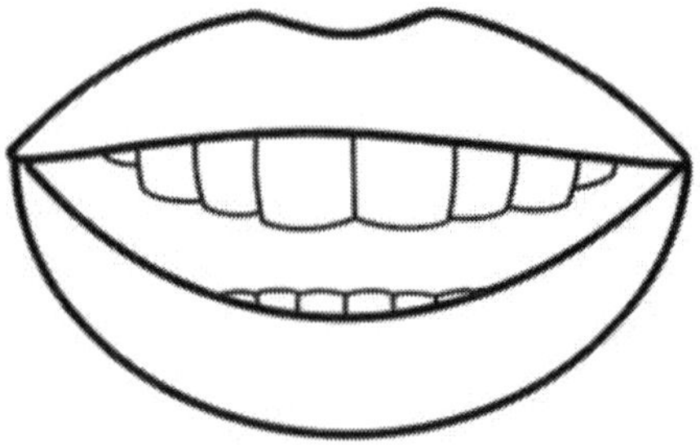

Handwriting 11: Long vowel u: **ew, ui, ue**

blue fruit glue drew suit suitcase

Trace **Write**

blue blue

fruit fruit

glue glue

drew drew

suit suit

suitcase suitcase

I drew blue fruit.

The suitcase has a suit.

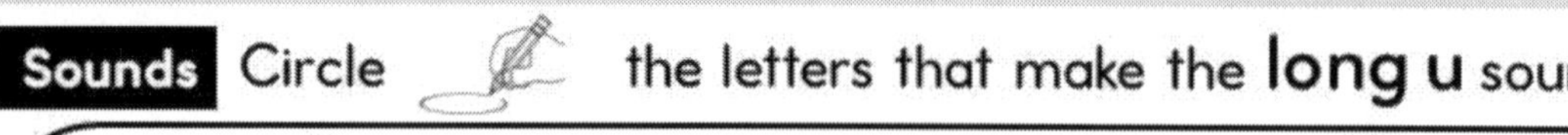

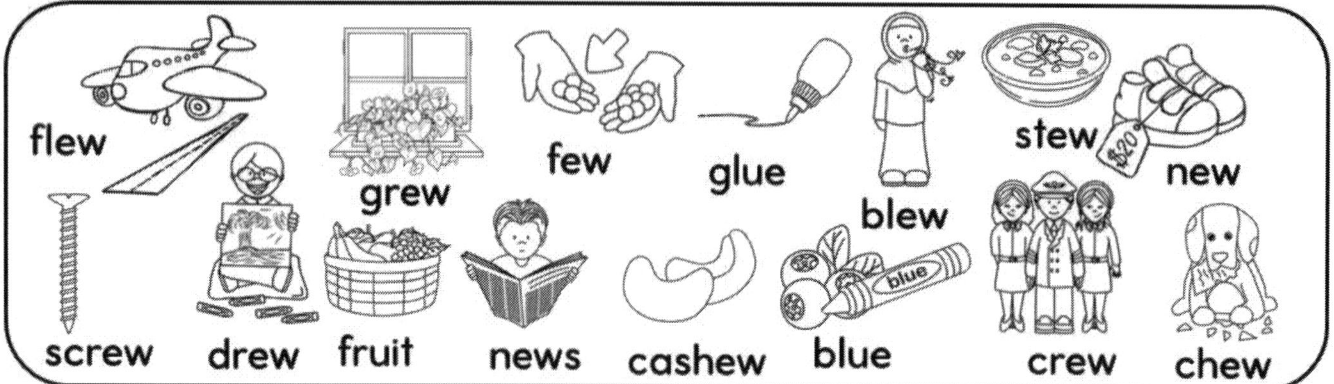

Read Words

few flew new news grew

drew crew screw fruit glue

blew blue stew chew cashew

Read Sentences Circle  the picture that matches the sentence.

The plant grew.

Chew the cashew nut.

I drew the crew.

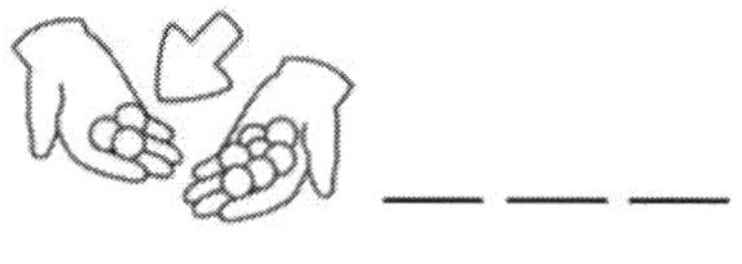 _ _ _

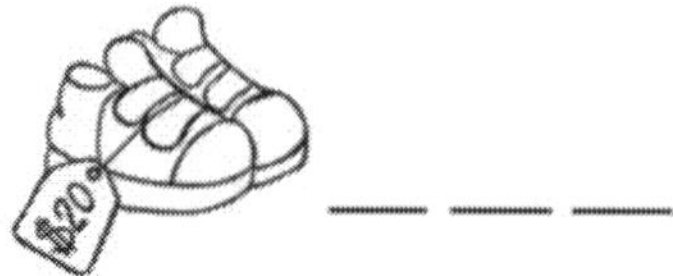 _ _ _

 _ _ _ _

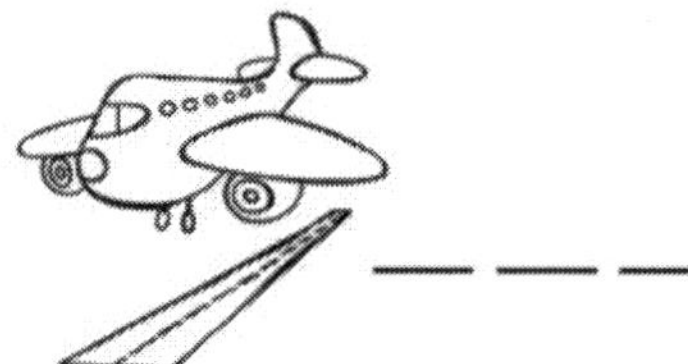 _ _ _ _

 _ _ _ _

 _ _ _ _

few, new, chew, flew, news, crew

The Plane

The pilot checks the plane. The pilot checks that the plane has fuel and checks the plane screws. The pilot gets onto the plane.

The crew has on suits. The crew has suitcases. The crew gets onto the flight. The crew tells what to do if there is a rescue.

The plane is up in the sky. Look out the window at the view! The crew gives out fruit and a few cashews. Then the crew puts stew on the tray.

The plane lands. The crew gets off. The pilot gets off. The pilot flew the plane to a new state.

screw plane suit flew fruit tray rescue pilot fuel truck crew suitcase window view few cashews stew

Who checks the plane?

What does the crew have on?

What does the crew give out?

Where did the plane land?

Vocabulary 11: Long vowel u: ew, ui, ue

I can see the ___.	That is _____.	I_____.
_ _ _ _	_ _ _ _	_ _ _ _
_ _ _ _	_ _ _	_ _ _ _
_ _ _ _ _ _	_ _ _ _	chew
_ _ _ _ _	a _ _ _	**It can _____.**
_ _ _ _	**Look at the _____.**	_ _ _ _
_ _ _ _	_ _ _ _	**I can _____.**
	_ _ _ _	_ _ _ _ _ _
	_ _ _ _ _	**It _____.**
	_ _ _ _	_ _ _ _
	_ _ _ _ _ _ _ _	_ _ _ _

Long and Short Vowel oo

Long **oo** oo zoo	Long **oo** oo school	Long **ou** ou soup
Long **ou** ou you	Short **oo** oo look	Short **oo** oo book

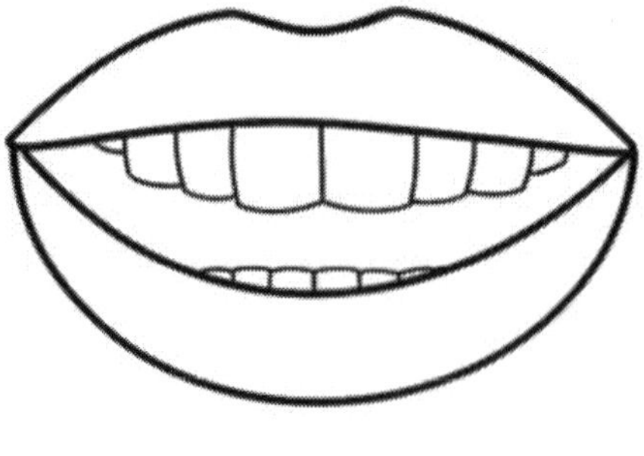

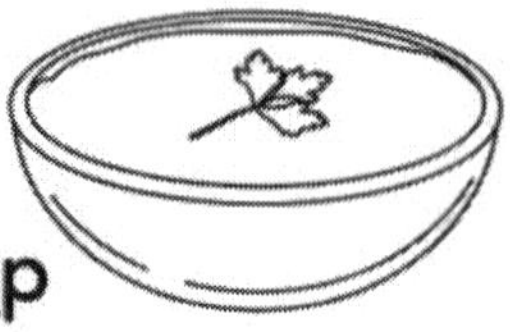

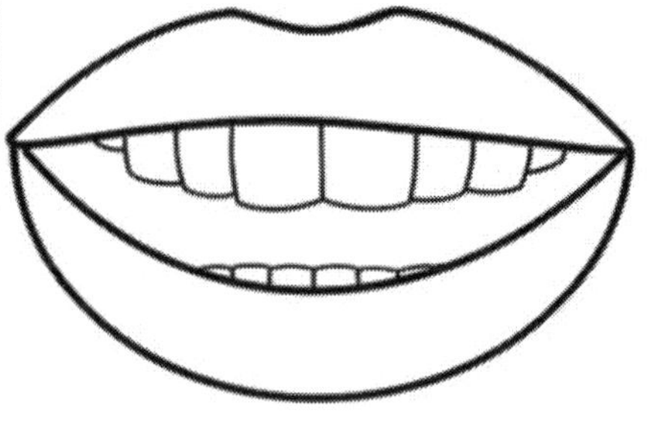

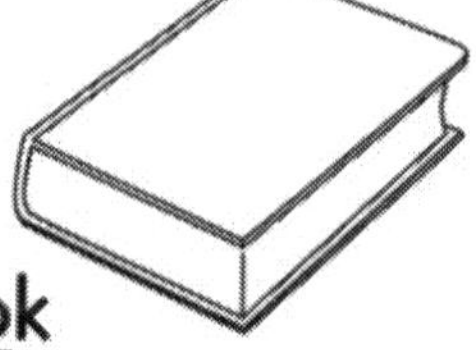

Handwriting 12: Long and Short oo: oo & ou

food  boots  school  you  soup  group

Trace Write

food food

roots roots

chew chew

fruit fruit

glue glue

few few

The group is at school.

The soup is food.

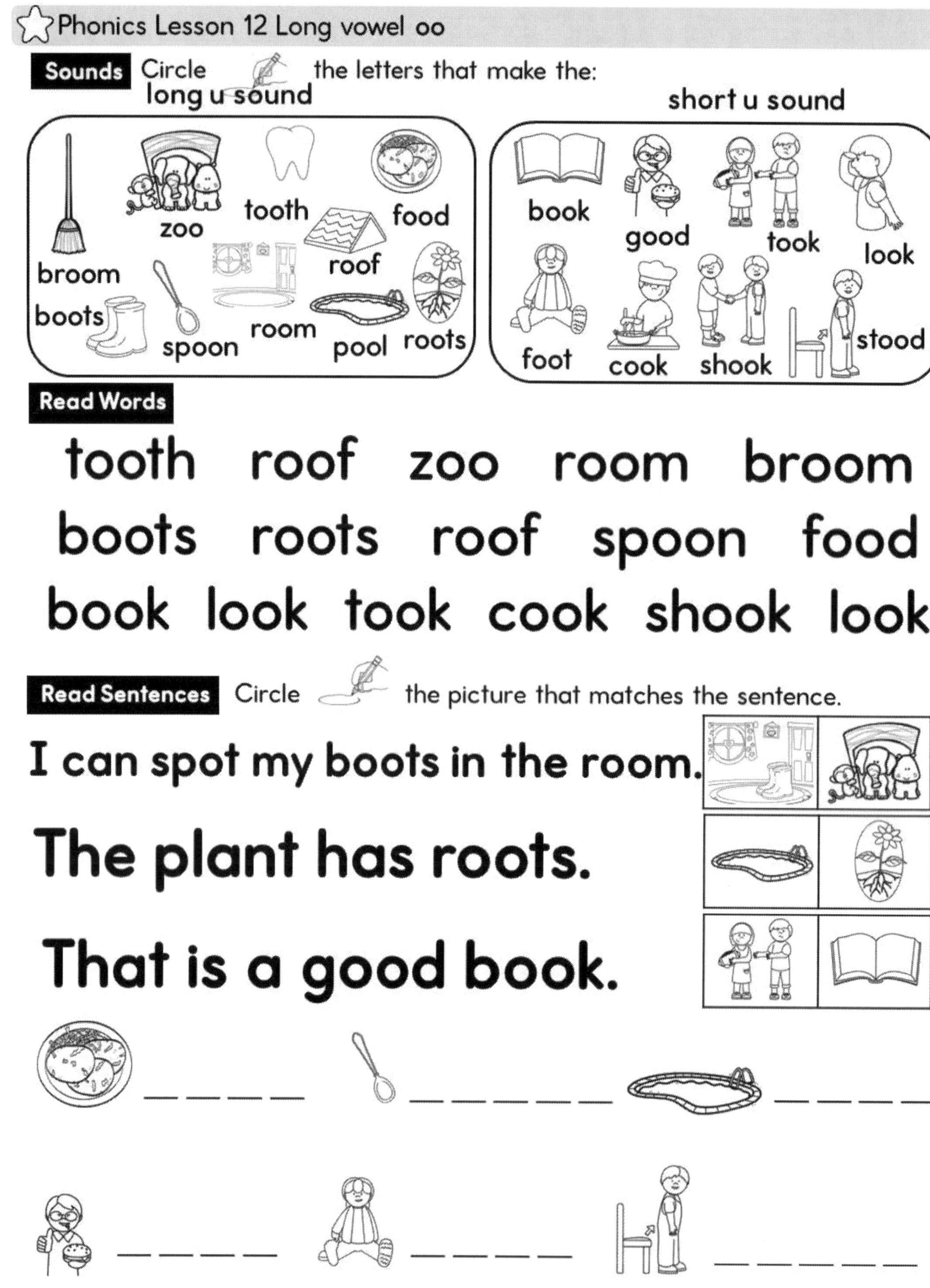
Sounds
Circle the letters that make the:
long u sound
short u sound
broom
zoo
tooth
food
roof
boots
spoon
room
pool
roots
book
good
took
look
foot
cook
shook
stood
Read Words
tooth roof zoo room broom
boots roots roof spoon food
book look took cook shook look
Read Sentences
Circle the picture that matches the sentence.
I can spot my boots in the room.
The plant has roots.
That is a good book.

The Zoo

The kids go to school. Then, at noon, they go to the zoo. The red group goes to a room with books. The blue group goes to look at roots. The green group looks at a big tooth. A man in boots gives the kids a toothbrush to brush the big tooth. It is a moose tooth. Then, the red group looks at grey seals. The blue group looks at ducks on a wood log.

Vocabulary 12: Long and short vowel oo: oo & ou

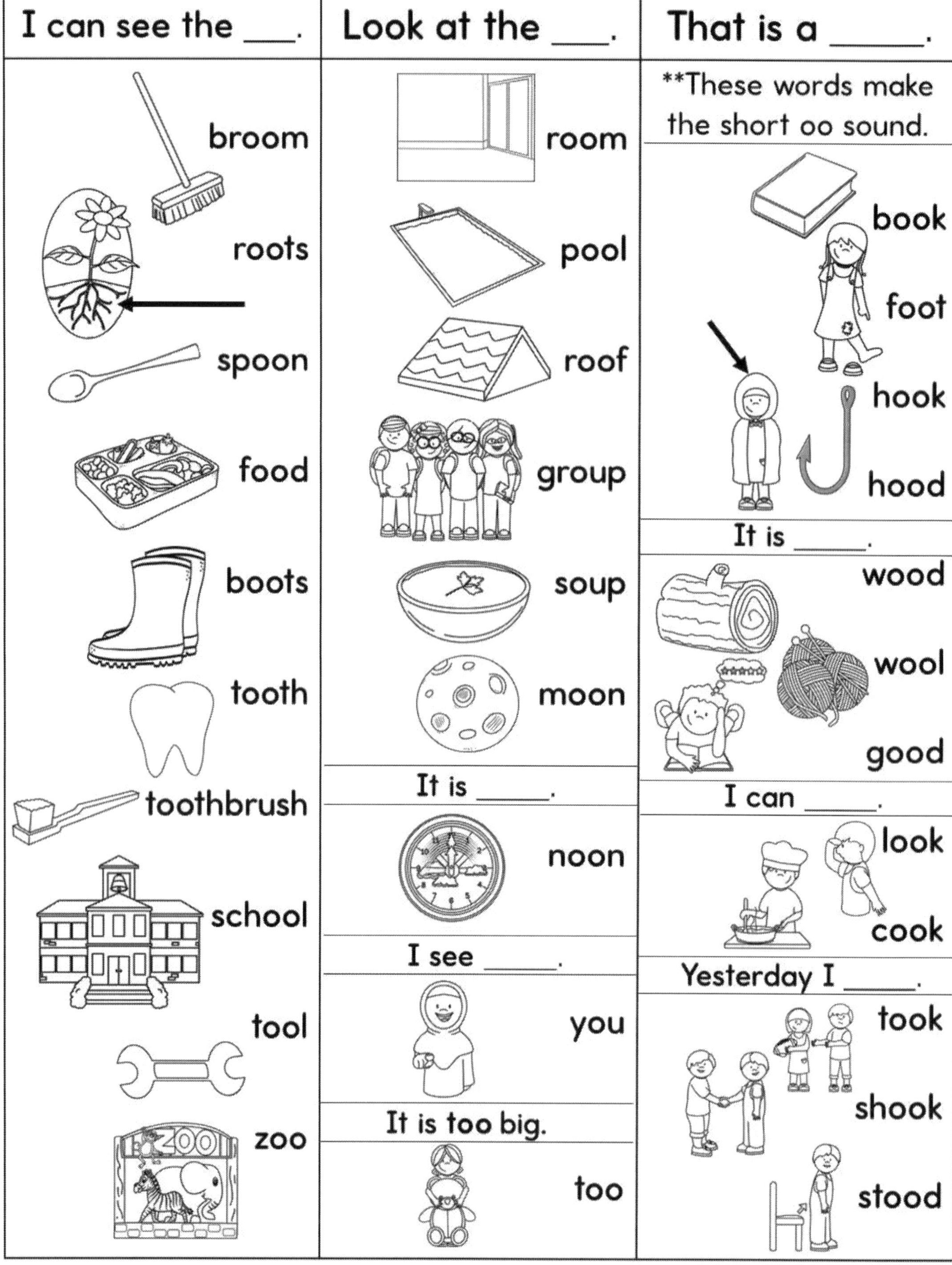

I can see the ___.	Look at the ___.	That is a _____.
broom	room	**These words make the short oo sound.
roots	pool	book
spoon	roof	foot
food	group	hook
boots	soup	hood
tooth	moon	It is _____.
toothbrush	It is _____.	wood
school	noon	wool
tool	I see _____.	good
zoo	you	I can _____.
	It is too big.	look
	too	cook
		Yesterday I _____.
		took
		shook
		stood

Vocabulary and Spelling 12: Long and Short oo: oo & ou

I can see the ___.	That is _____.	I_____.
_ _ _ _ _	_ _ _ _	*These words make the short oo sound.
_ _ _ _ _	_ _ _ _	_ _ _ _
_ _ _ _ _	_ _ _ _ _	_ _ _ _
_ _ _ _	_ _ _ _	_ _ _ _
_ _ _ _ _	_ _ _ _	_ _ _ _
_ _ _ _ _	**It is _____.**	**It is _____.**
_ _ _ _ _ _ _ _ _ _	_ _ _ _	_ _ _ _
_ _ _ _ _ _	**I see _____.**	_ _ _ _
_ _ _	_ _ _	_ _ _ _
	It is too big.	**I can _____.**
	_ _ _	_ _ _ _
		_ _ _ _
		Yesterday I _____.
		_ _ _ _
		_ _ _ _ _
		_ _ _ _ _

Soft c and g

comes before e, i, y

s c dance	s c city	s c juicy
j g gem	j g giant	j g gym

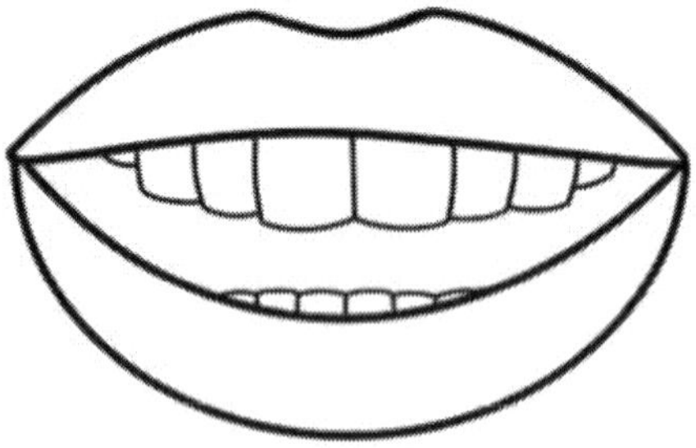

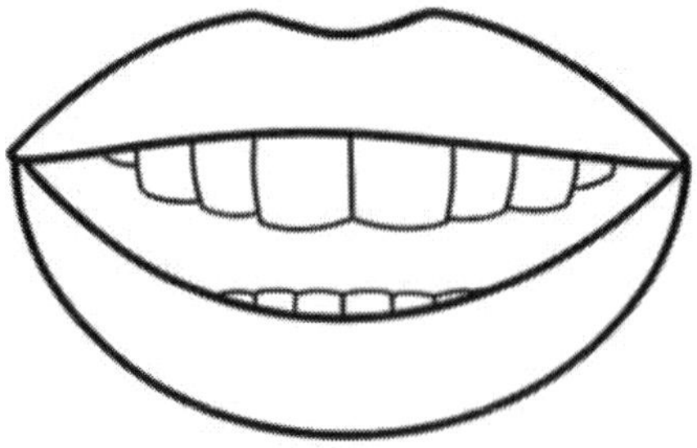

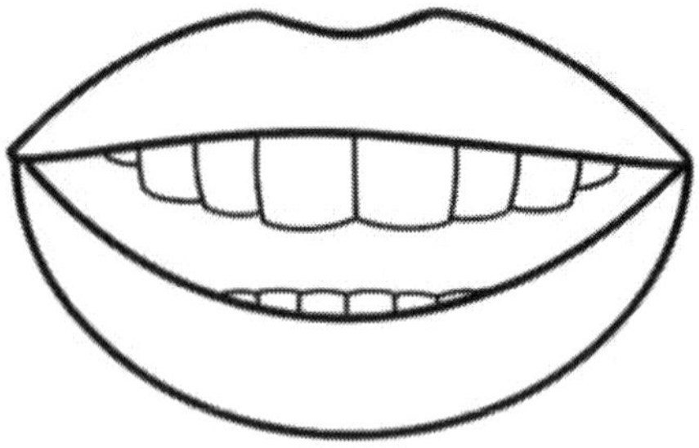

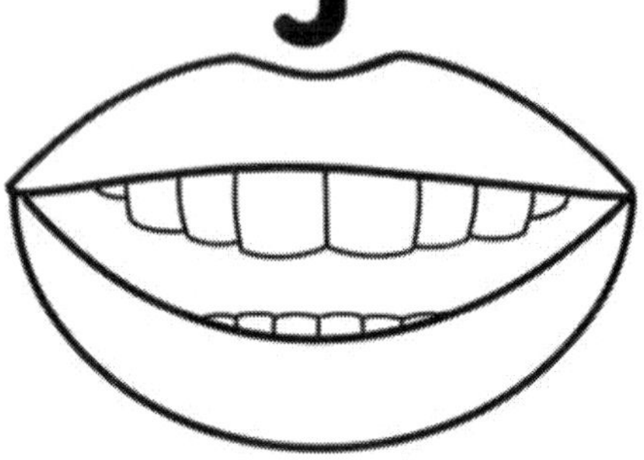

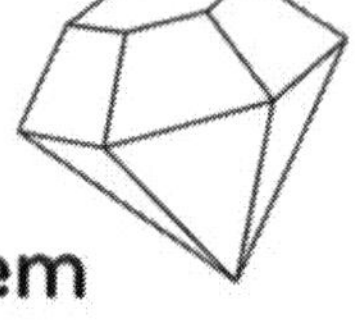

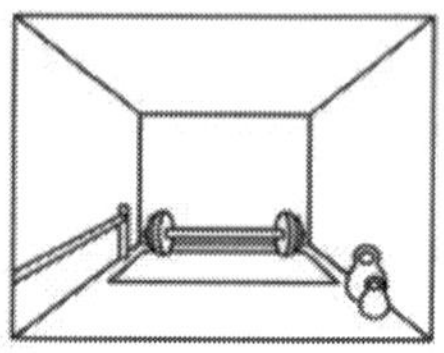

Handwriting 13: Long vowel soft c and g

pencil juice ice rice city bicycle

Trace Write

pencil pencil

juice juice

ice ice

rice rice

city city

bicycle bicycle

The juice has ice in it.

The bicycle is in the city.

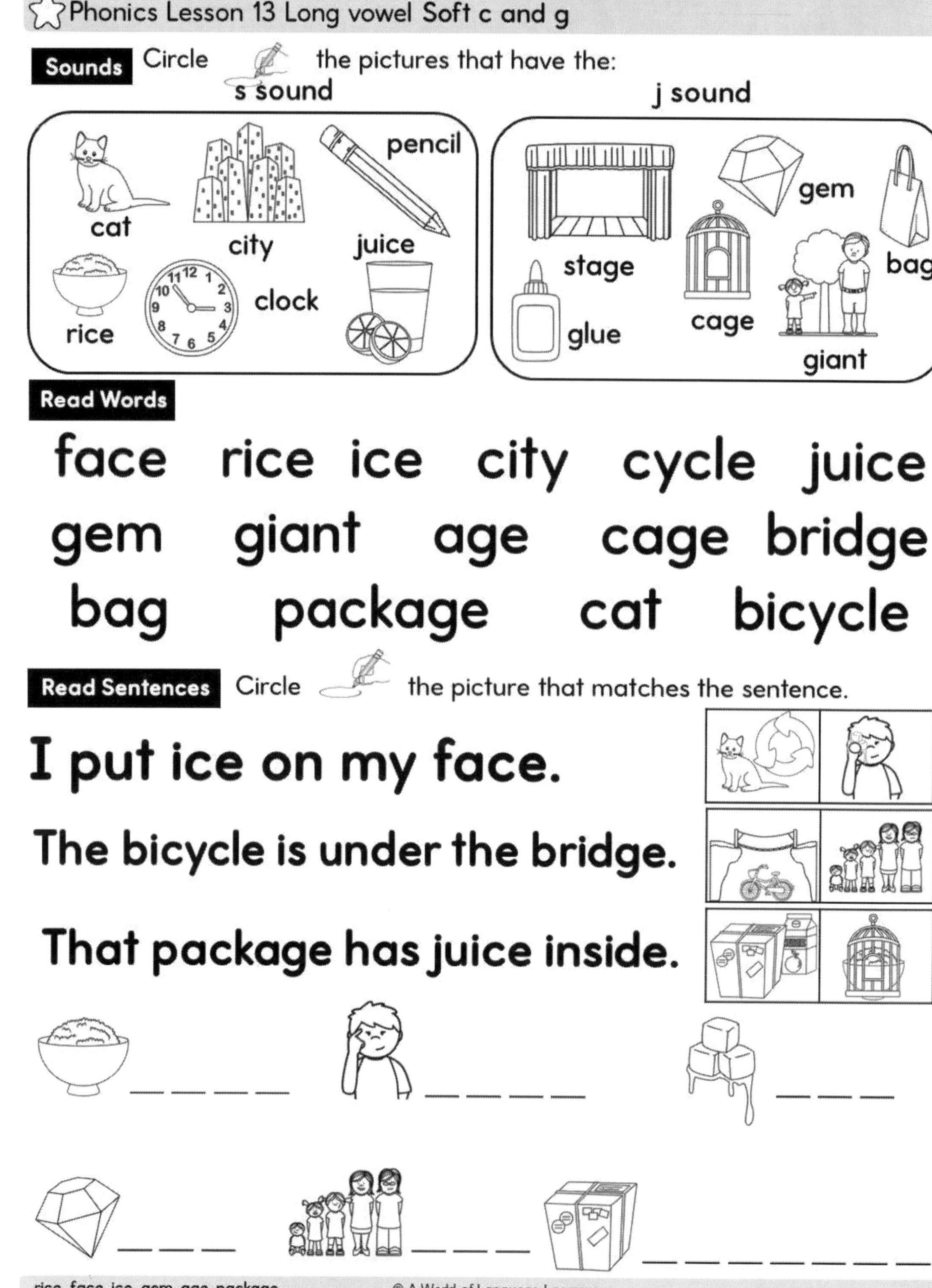

rice, face, ice, gem, age, package

The Dance

Jene is excited to dance. She walks to the center of the stage and dances. Then she gets onto a bicycle and rides over the bridge. Jene puts on a fancy dress. The dress has lace. She puts on a gem necklace. She meets Grace in the city. They celebrate with fruit juice that has ice and nice hot rice.

Vocabulary 13: Long vowels: Soft c and g

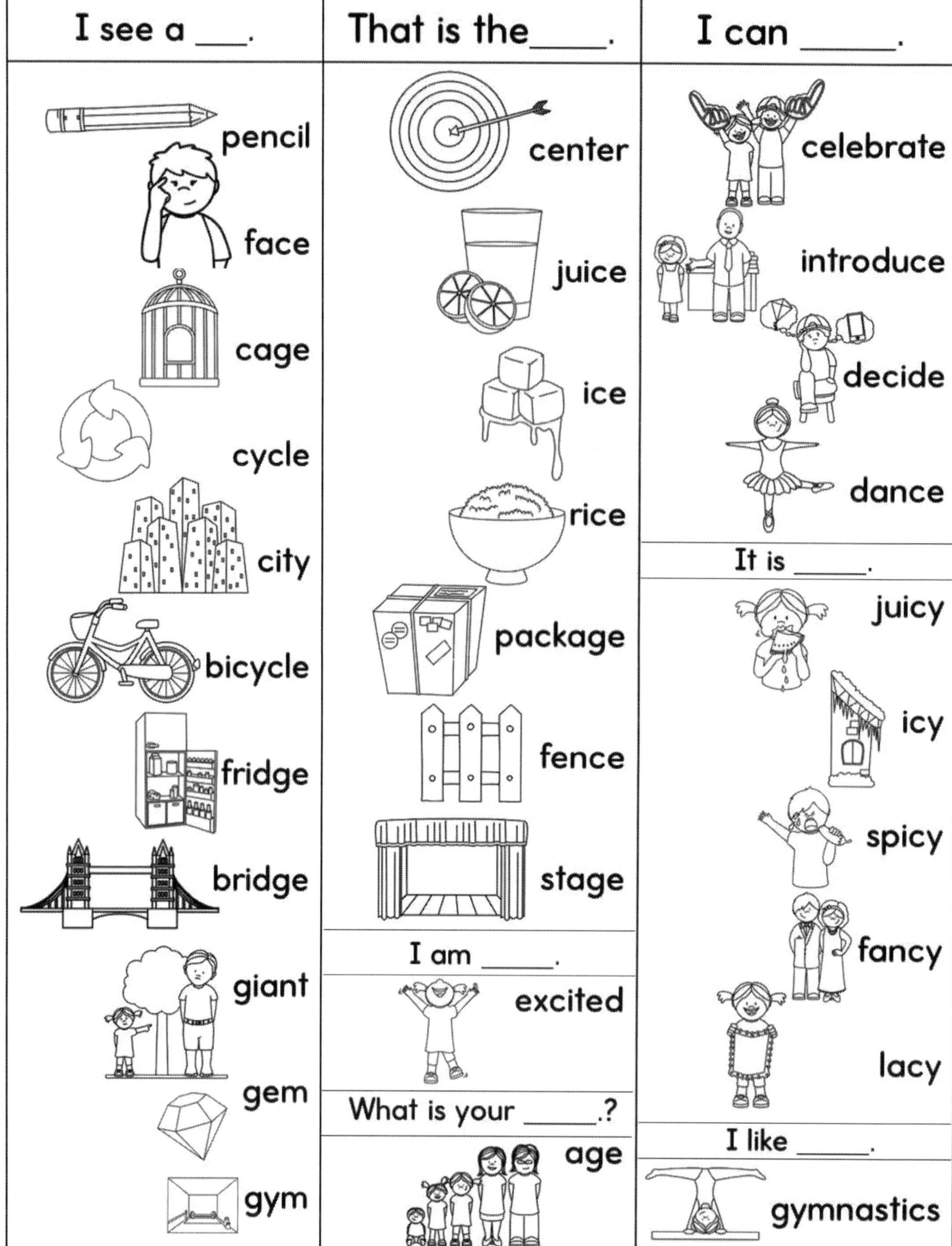

I see a ___.	That is the____.	I can _____.
_ _ _ _ _ _	_ _ _ _ _ _	_ _ _ _ _ _ _ _
_ _ _ _	_ _ _ _ _	_ _ _ _ _ _ _ _
_ _ _ _	_ _ _	_ _ _ _ _ _
_ _ _ _ _	_ _ _ _	_ _ _ _ _
_ _ _ _	_ _ _ _ _ _ _	**It is _____.**
_ _ _ _ _ _ _	_ _ _ _ _	_ _ _ _ _
_ _ _ _ _ _	_ _ _ _ _	_ _ _
_ _ _ _ _ _	**I am _____.**	_ _ _ _ _
_ _ _ _ _	_ _ _ _ _ _ _	_ _ _ _ _
_ _ _	**What is your _____?**	_ _ _ _
_ _ _	_ _ _	_ _ _ _ _ _ _ _ _ _

Terms of Use

Thank you for purchasing this product.
The contents are the property of Ellie Tiemann and licensed to you only for classroom/personal use as a single user. I retain the copyright, and reserve all rights to this product.

You may not claim this work as your own, giveaway, or sell any portion of this product. You may not share this product anywhere on the internet or on school share sites.

Find more teaching resources at

https://www.teacherspayteachers.com/Store/A-World-Of-Language-Learners

Get weekly tips and find out about teaching resources at

https://www.aworldoflanguagelearners.com/newsletter/

Made in the USA
Middletown, DE
29 August 2024

59955306R00055